AQA History

AS
Unit 2

The Impact of Chairman Mao: China, 1946–1976

Exclusively endorsed by AQA

Robert Whitfield

Series editor
Sally Waller

Nelson Thornes

Published in 2008 by:
Nelson Thornes Ltd
Delta Place
27 Bath Road
CHELTENHAM
GL53 7TH
United Kingdom

08 09 10 11 12 / 10 9 8 7 6 5 4 3 2 1

A catalogue record for this book is available from the British Library

978-0-7487-8264-2

Illustrations by: Bob Moulder (c/o Graham Cameron Illustration), David Russell Illustration

Page make-up by Thomson Digital

Printed in Great Britain by Scotprint

Contents

AQA introduction

Nelson Thornes and AQA

Nelson Thornes has worked in collaboration with AQA to ensure that this book offers you the best support for your AS or A level course and helps you to prepare for your exams. The partnership means that you can be confident that the range of learning, teaching and assessment practice materials has been checked by the senior examining team at AQA before formal approval, and is closely matched to the requirements of your specification.

How to use this book

This book covers the specification for your course and is arranged in a sequence approved by AQA.

The features in this book include:

Timeline

Key events are outlined at the beginning of the book. The events are colour-coded so you can clearly see the categories of change.

Learning objectives

At the beginning of each section you will find a list of learning objectives that contain targets linked to the requirements of the specification.

Key chronology

A short list of dates usually with a focus on a specific event or legislation.

Key profile

The profile of a key person you should be aware of to fully understand the period in question.

Key terms

Terms that you will need to be able to define and understand.

Did you know?

Interesting information to bring the subject under discussion to life.

Exploring the detail

Information to put further context around the subject under discussion.

A closer look

An in-depth look at a theme, person or event to deepen your understanding. Activities around the extra information may be included.

Sources

Sources to reinforce topics or themes and may provide fact or opinion. They may be quotations from historical works, contemporaries of the period or photographs.

Cross-reference

Links to related content within the book which may offer more detail on the subject in question.

Activity

Various activity types to provide you with different challenges and opportunities to demonstrate both the content and skills you are learning. Some can be worked on individually, some as part of group work and some are designed to specifically 'stretch and challenge'.

Question

Questions to prompt further discussion on the topic under consideration and are an aid to revision.

Summary questions

Summary questions at the end of each chapter to test your knowledge and allow you to demonstrate your understanding.

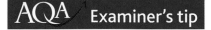 **Examiner's tip**

Hints from AQA examiners to help you with your study and to prepare for your examination.

 **Examination-style questions**

Questions in the style that you can expect in your examination.

AQA examination questions are reproduced by permission of the Assessment and Qualifications Alliance.

Learning outcomes

Learning outcomes at the end of each section remind you what you should know having completed the chapters in that section.

Web links in the book

Because Nelson Thornes is not responsible for third party content online, there may be some changes to this material that are beyond our control. In order for us to ensure that the links referred to in the book are as up to date and stable as possible, the websites provided are usually homepages with supporting instructions on how to reach the relevant pages if necessary.

Please let us know at **webadmin@nelsonthornes.com** if you find a link that does not work and we will do our best to correct this at reprint, or to list an alternative site.

Introduction to the History series

When Bruce Bogtrotter in Roald Dahl's *Matilda* was challenged to eat a huge chocolate cake, he just opened his mouth and ploughed in, taking bite after bite and lump after lump until the cake was gone and he was feeling decidedly sick. The picture is not dissimilar to that of some A level history students. They are attracted to history because of its inherent appeal but, when faced with a bulging file and a forthcoming examination, their enjoyment evaporates. They try desperately to cram their brains with an assortment of random facts and subsequently prove unable to control the outpouring of their ill-digested material in the examination.

The books in this series are designed to help students and teachers avoid this feeling of overload and examination panic by breaking down the AQA history specification in such a way that it is easily absorbed. Above all, they are designed to retain and promote students' enthusiasm for history by avoiding a dreary rehash of dates and events. Each book is divided into sections, closely matched to those given in the specification, and the content is further broken down into chapters that present the historical material in a lively and attractive form, offering guidance on the key terms, events and issues, and blending thought-provoking activities and questions in a way designed to advance students' understanding. By encouraging students to think for themselves and to share their ideas with others, as well as helping them to develop the knowledge and skills they will need to pass their examination, this book should ensure that students' learning remains a pleasure rather than an endurance test.

To make the most of what this book provides, students will need to develop efficient study skills from the start and it is worth spending some time considering what these involve:

- Good organisation of material in a subject-specific file. Organised notes help develop an organised brain and sensible filing ensures time is not wasted hunting for misplaced material. This book uses cross-references to indicate where material in one chapter has relevance to material in another. Students are advised to adopt the same technique.

- A sensible approach to note-making. Students are often too ready to copy large chunks of material from printed books or to download sheaves of printouts from the internet. This series is designed to encourage students to think about the notes they collect and to undertake research with a particular purpose in mind. The activities encourage students to pick out information that is relevant to the issue being addressed and to avoid making notes on material that is not properly understood.

- Taking time to think, which is by far the most important component of study. By encouraging students to think before they write or speak, be it for a written answer, presentation or class debate, students should learn to form opinions and make judgements based on the accumulation of evidence. These are the skills that the examiner will be looking for in the final examination. The beauty of history is that there is rarely a right or wrong answer so, with sufficient evidence, one student's view will count for as much as the next.

Unit 2

Unit 2 promotes the study of significant periods of history in depth. Although the span of years may appear short, the chosen topics are centred on periods of change that raise specific historical issues and they therefore provide an opportunity for students to study in some depth the interrelationships between ideas, individuals, circumstances and other factors that lead to major developments. Appreciating the dynamics of change, and balancing the degree of change against elements of continuity, make for a fascinating and worthwhile study. Students are also required to analyse consequences and draw conclusions about the issues these studies raise. Such themes are, of course, relevant to an understanding of the present and, through such an historical investigation, students will be guided towards a greater appreciation of the world around them today, as well as develop their understanding of the past.

Unit 2 is tested by a 1 hour 30 minute paper containing three questions. The first question is compulsory and based on sources, while the remaining two, of which students will need to choose one, are two-part questions as described in Table 1. Plentiful sources are included throughout this book to give students some familiarity with contemporary and historiographical material, and activities and suggestions are provided to enable students to develop the required examination skills. Students should familiarise themselves with the question breakdown, additional hints and marking criteria given below before attempting any of the practice examination-style questions at the end of each section.

Answers will be marked according to a scheme based on 'levels of response'. This means that the answer will be assessed according to which level best matches the historical skills displayed, taking both knowledge and understanding into account. All students should have a copy of these criteria and need to use them wisely.

Table 1 *Unit 2: style of questions and marks available*

Unit 2	Question	Marks	Question type	Question stem	Hints for students
Question 1 based on three sources of c.300–350 words in total	(a)	12	This question involves the comparison of two sources	Explain how far the views in Source B differ from those in Source A in relation to…	Take pains to avoid simply writing out what each source says with limited direct comment. Instead, you should try to find two or three points of comparison and illustrate these with reference to the sources. You should also look for any underlying similarities. In your conclusion, you will need to make it clear exactly 'how far' the views differ
Question 1	(b)	24	This requires use of the sources and own knowledge and asks for an explanation that shows awareness that issues and events can provoke differing views and explanations	How far… How important was… How successful…	This answer needs to be planned as you will need to develop an argument in your answer and show balanced judgement. Try to set out your argument in the introduction and, as you develop your ideas through your paragraphs, support your opinions with detailed evidence. Your conclusion should flow naturally and provide supported judgement. The sources should be used as 'evidence' throughout your answer. Do ensure you refer to them all
Question 2 and 3	(a)	12	This question is focused on a narrow issue within the period studied and requires an explanation	Explain why…	Make sure you explain 'why', not 'how', and try to order your answer in a way that shows you understand the inter-linkage of factors and which are the most important. You should try to reach an overall judgement/conclusion
Question 2 and 3	(b)	24	This question is broader and asks for analysis and explanation with appropriate judgement. The question requires an awareness of debate over issues	A quotation in the form of a judgement on a key development or issue will be given and candidates asked: Explain why you agree or disagree with this view	This answer needs to be planned as you will need to show balanced judgement. Try to think of points that agree and disagree and decide which way you will argue. Set out your argument in the introduction and support it through your paragraphs, giving the alternative picture too but showing why your view is the more convincing. Your conclusion should flow naturally from what you have written

Marking criteria

Question 1(a)

Level 1 Answers either briefly paraphrase/describe the content of the two sources or identify simple comparison(s) between the sources. Skills of written communication will be weak. *(0–2 marks)*

Level 2 Responses will compare the views expressed in the two sources and identify some differences and/or similarities. There may be some limited own knowledge. Answers will be coherent but weakly expressed. *(3–6 marks)*

Level 3 Responses will compare the views expressed in the two sources, identifying differences **and** similarities and using own knowledge to explain and evaluate these. Answers will, for the most part, be clearly expressed. *(7–9 marks)*

Level 4 Responses will make a developed comparison between the views expressed in the two sources **and** own knowledge will apply to evaluate and to demonstrate a good contextual understanding. Answers will, for the most part, show good skills of written communication. *(10–12 marks)*

Question 1(b)

Level 1 Answers may be based on sources or on own knowledge alone, or they may comprise an undeveloped mixture of the two. They may contain some descriptive material which is only loosely linked to the focus of the question or they may address only a part of the question. Alternatively, there may be some explicit comment with little, if any, appropriate support. Answers are likely to be generalised and assertive. There will be little, if any, awareness of differing historical interpretations. The response will be limited in development and skills of written communication will be weak. *(0–6 marks)*

Level 2 Answers may be based on sources or on own knowledge alone, or they may contain a mixture of the two. They may be almost entirely descriptive with few explicit links to the focus of the question. Alternatively, they may contain some explicit comment with relevant but limited support. They will display limited understanding of differing historical interpretations. Answers will be coherent but weakly expressed and/or poorly structured. *(7–11 marks)*

Level 3 Answers will show a developed understanding of the demands of the question using evidence from **both** the sources **and** own knowledge. They will provide some assessment backed by relevant and appropriately selected evidence, but they will lack depth and/or balance. There will be some understanding of varying historical interpretations. Answers will, for the most part, be clearly expressed and show some organisation in the presentation of material. *(12–16 marks)*

Level 4 Answers will show explicit understanding of the demands of the question. They will develop a balanced argument backed by a good range of appropriately selected evidence from the sources and own knowledge, and a good understanding of historical interpretations. Answers will, for the most part, show organisation and good skills of written communication. *(17–21 marks)*

Level 5 Answers will be well focused and closely argued. The arguments will be supported by precisely selected evidence from the sources and own knowledge, incorporating well-developed understanding of historical interpretations and debate. Answers will, for the most part, be carefully organised and fluently written, using appropriate vocabulary. *(22–24 marks)*

Question 2(a) and 3(a)

Level 1 Answers will contain either some descriptive material which is only loosely linked to the focus of the question or some explicit comment with little, if any, appropriate support. Answers are likely to be generalised and assertive. The response will be limited in development and skills of written communication will be weak. *(0–2 marks)*

Level 2 Answers will demonstrate some knowledge and understanding of the demands of the question. They will either be almost entirely descriptive with few explicit links to the question **or** they provide some explanations backed by evidence that is limited in range and/or depth. Answers will be coherent but weakly expressed and/or poorly structured. *(3–6 marks)*

Level 3 Answers will demonstrate good understanding of the demands of the question providing relevant explanations backed by appropriately selected information, although this may not be full or comprehensive. Answers will, for the most part, be clearly expressed and show some organisation in the presentation of material. *(7–9 marks)*

Level 4 Answers will be well focused, identifying a range of specific explanations backed by precise evidence and demonstrating good understanding of the connections and links between events/issues. Answers will, for the most part, be well written and organised. *(10–12 marks)*

Question 2(b) and 3(b)

Level 1 Answers may **either** contain some descriptive material which is only loosely linked to the focus of the question **or** they may address only a limited part of the period of the question. Alternatively, there may be some explicit comment with little, if any, appropriate support. Answers are likely to be generalised and assertive. There will be little, if any, awareness of different historical interpretations. The response will be limited in development and skills of written communication will be weak. *(0–6 marks)*

Level 2 Answers will show some understanding of the demands of the question. They will either be almost entirely descriptive with few explicit links to the question **or** they contain some explicit comment with relevant but limited support. They will display limited understanding of differing historical interpretations. Answers will be coherent but weakly expressed and/or poorly structured. *(7–11 marks)*

Level 3 Answers will show a developed understanding of the demands of the question. They will provide some assessment, backed by relevant and appropriately selected evidence, but they will lack depth and/or balance. There will be some understanding of varying historical interpretations. Answers will, for the most part, be clearly expressed and show some organisation in the presentation of material. *(12–16 marks)*

Level 4 Answers will show explicit understanding of the demands of the question. They will develop a balanced argument backed by a good range of appropriately selected evidence and a good understanding of historical interpretations. Answers will, for the most part, show organisation and good skills of written communication. *(17–21 marks)*

Level 5 Answers will be well focused and closely argued. The arguments will be supported by precisely selected evidence leading to a relevant conclusion/judgement, incorporating well-developed understanding of historical interpretations and debate. Answers will, for the most part, be carefully organised and fluently written, using appropriate vocabulary. *(22–24 marks)*

Introduction to this book

Mao Zedong, usually referred to as Chairman Mao, dominated China from October 1949, when he led the Chinese Communist Party to power, until his death in 1976. During those 37 years, Mao was the subject of a growing personality cult that was promoted not only by the Chairman himself but also by the rest of the Communist Party leadership. Mao was the 'Great Helmsman' who was steering the revolutionary course for the People's Republic of China on its voyage towards a communist utopia. His image was everywhere in China in the form of posters, photographs and statues. His speeches and poems were reproduced in newspapers and his writings became required reading for all. Mao Zedong Thought, which in the 1960s was published in the *Little Red Book*, became the guiding principles for political action and was enshrined in the Chinese constitution. Although Mao did not rule China alone and his power and influence were greater at some times than at others, it is nevertheless true that he had the most profound impact on every area of Chinese society. The China that he passed on to his successors was a very different country from that into which he had been born.

Mao Zedong was born in 1893 in Hunan province. In later years, he would make much of his humble peasant origins although, in fact, his father was a well-to-do grain merchant and farmer. Mao therefore had a somewhat more comfortable upbringing than the majority of Chinese peasants, whose 'reward' for a life of back-breaking labour was extreme poverty. Mao showed himself to be rebellious in his youth, trying to run away from home at the age of 10 in protest against his father's beatings and refusing to enter into an arranged marriage against his father's wishes. In doing so, he was taking his first steps towards rejecting the traditional Confucian values on which Chinese family and social relationships were based. China in the 1890s and early 1900s was experiencing a serious social and political crisis that was causing young people to question old certainties and to embrace new ideas, many of which were reaching China from the West.

Crisis in China

Since the 17th century, China had been ruled by the Qing dynasty. Over many thousands of years the Chinese had demonstrated their superiority over Western nations in many ways. The use of a standardised written language, the development of complex systems of government and education, and the invention of printing and gunpowder all occurred in China long before these things were developed or discovered in western Europe. However, by the 19th century China had fallen behind the West in the development of technology, particularly in weapons. Therefore, when Western powers such as Britain began to use force to persuade a reluctant Chinese government to open up its ports to trade with foreign merchants, Chinese resistance was ineffective and futile. By the 1890s, the Chinese Empire was being carved up between various European powers

Exploring the detail

Confucian values

Confucius lived in the 5th century BC but his teachings dominated China until the modern era. He stressed the value of harmony in all things. This should be achieved through respect for legitimate authority, including that of a parent or government, as long as that government ruled wisely and did not abuse power. The philosophy of Confucius is expressed in the saying 'Reform yourself, then arrange your family and so pacify the world.'

Exploring the detail

Western influence in China

In the 1839–42 Opium War, Britain defeated China and forced the Emperor to open some Chinese ports to trade with the outside world. Britain also took control of the island of Hong Kong. Another defeat for China at the hands of Britain and France in 1858 led to the opening up of more Chinese ports. The foreigners who took up residence in China demanded that they should still be subject to the laws of their own countries, not to Chinese law, so 'extra-territorial courts' by foreign powers were set up.

and Japan. Foreign companies were building railways, factories, mines and ports to exploit China's natural resources. Foreign soldiers were guarding foreign bases on Chinese soil. Foreign residents in China refused to be bound by Chinese laws and would only submit to justice administered by their own 'extra-territorial courts'. Christian missionaries were seeking to convert Chinese people and building hospitals and schools to extend their influence. These humiliations were deeply resented by most Chinese, while the inability of the Emperor to resist growing foreign influence in China severely undermined his authority. A growing nationalist movement among the educated elite sought not only to restore China's national pride but also to modernise the system of government as a first step towards removing foreign influence.

■ The end of the Qing dynasty

Resentment at growing foreign influence coincided with a serious economic and political crisis in China. A rising population put pressure on food supplies and caused **inflation**. This was made worse by China's increasing reliance on imports of foreign-made goods, which led to a weakening of the country's financial position. Widespread corruption among local and provincial government officials meant that a large portion of tax revenues did not reach central government, further weakening its financial position. There had been a number of revolts against imperial rule during the 19th century, culminating in the Boxer Rising of 1900 which was primarily a revolt against foreign influence but also threatened to undermine the authority of the Emperor. Pressure for change, although resisted by the Dowager Empress Cixi and her conservative allies, resulted in constitutional reform and the creation of a new professional army in the early 20th century. Such reforms, however, arrived too late to save the dynasty. Growing unrest culminated in an uprising in 1911 which led to the abdication of the Emperor and the setting up of the Chinese Republic.

Yuan Shikai

After the fall of imperial rule, effective power in China was in the hands of the new army and its Commander-in-Chief, Yuan Shikai. Although Yuan at first allowed political parties to be established and elections to be held for a new House of Representatives (parliament), he was not prepared to share power with elected politicians. After the new nationalist National People's Party (Guomindang), led by Sun Yat-sen, won the largest share of the vote, Yuan Shikai outlawed political parties and had himself declared Emperor in 1915. When he died in 1916, he left no clear successor and no stable form of government in China. The result was that for the next 10 years China had no effective system of central government. Instead, provincial **warlords** governed different parts of the country. Wars between rival warlords left areas devastated. Heavy taxes were imposed on the peasants to pay for the warlords' growing armies. Any resistance was put down with brutal force. Internally weakened, China was in no position to resist when, in 1919, the victorious Western Allies in the First World War granted former German-held territory in China to Japan. Student demonstrations against China's treatment at the hands of the Western Allies, held in Beijing's Tiananmen Square on 4 May 1919, failed to have any impact on the actions of the Western powers. Once again, China's impotence had been underlined.

■ Exploring the detail

The Qing dynasty

The last in a long line of dynasties to rule China, the Qing dynasty was established by Manchu conquerors from the north in the 17th century, hence they are sometimes referred to as the Manchu emperors. During the 18th century, China had prospered under their rule.

■ Key terms

Inflation: an increase in prices. Inflation is usually caused when goods are in short supply.

Warlords: powerful local leaders who had their own armies. They ruled their territories as independent kingdoms.

■ Exploring the detail

The May 4th Movement

At the Versailles Peace Conference in 1919, the Allied powers (Britain, France and the USA) had decided that Japan, which had joined the alliance in the First World War, should be rewarded for its support by being allowed to take over former German territory in China. This was regarded in China as another national humiliation and provoked violent protests in Beijing. This led to the spread of a nationwide student protest movement, known as the May 4th Movement, which was dedicated to change and the rebirth of China as a proud, independent nation. The movement could not agree, however, on exactly which changes should be made.

Did you know?

Communism and the Comintern

Communism is the political theory that argues for the abolition of private property and for all property to be owned communally. The Russian Revolution of 1917 had led to the creation of the world's first communist state. The Communist International (Comintern) had been established by the government in Russia (later the Soviet Union) to spread communist ideas and build communist political parties in other countries.

Key term

Nationalism: Nationalists believe in the concept of nationhood, usually defined by a common language and common culture. They argue that the members of a nation should belong to the same State and that the State should be independent of foreign control or influence.

Communists and Nationalists

During the early 1920s, those Chinese who wanted a strong, united China, free of foreign interference, had a choice between two main political parties. The Guomindang (GMD), led by Sun Yat-sen until his death in 1925, was the larger and more established party. Its aims were summarised in its Three Principles: **Nationalism**, democracy and the people's livelihood. With wealthy backers among China's businessmen and landlords, and the creation of a new National Revolutionary Army (NRA), the GMD was fast becoming the dominant party in China in the early 1920s. In 1921, the Communist Party of China (CPC) was also established, led by Chen Duxiu but heavily influenced by Russian advisers sent to China by the Communist International (Comintern). The young Mao Zedong was an early recruit to the new party and began to attract attention for his work in building Communist Party membership in his home area of Hunan. Although CPC membership grew rapidly – by 1926 it had 30,000 members – it was still a small minority party and, following the insistence of its Russian advisers, it worked closely with the GMD. In its early years, the CPC concentrated on recruiting industrial workers in cities such as Shanghai, although Mao also carried out propaganda work among peasants.

Key profile

Chen Duxiu

Chen Duxiu (1879–1942) was a radical intellectual who was involved in the May 4th Movement in 1919. He was one of the founders of the CPC in 1921 and its General Secretary from 1921 to 1927. He later broke with the CPC and joined an opposition group.

The White Terror

In 1926 the GMD, by now led by Chiang Kai-shek, decided to launch a military campaign to break the power of the warlords in northern China. In a short but bitterly fought campaign, the NRA took control of the Yangzi River basin and the city of Nanjing in central China. The campaign continued in 1927–8 until, by the end of 1928, Chiang and the GMD were in control over the whole of China from Guangzhou in the south to Manchuria in the north. In the early stages of the campaign, cooperation with the CPC was helpful to the GMD. Communist propaganda among the peasants led to many revolts, which undermined the warlords' power from within. However, cooperation with the Communists also caused problems for the GMD because its wealthy backers (businessmen and landlords) were vigorously opposed to working with a party that was agitating workers to strike and peasants to revolt. In 1927, therefore, Chiang decided to end cooperation with the Communists and destroy the CPC. In April 1927, NRA forces in Shanghai, working closely with criminal gangs, massacred the Communists and their supporters in the city's trades union movement. It has been estimated that between 5,000 and 10,000 people were killed. Similar anti-communist massacres, often referred to as the White Terror, were carried out by GMD forces in other cities, including Guangzhou. Attempts by Communists to start their own uprisings, for example in Nanchang, were easily and ruthlessly crushed.

Chiang Kai-shek

Chiang Kai-shek (1887–1975), the son of a salt merchant, came from a well-to-do middle-class family. Educated in China and Japan, he rose to prominence in the 1920s as a military leader in the Guomindang. He was sent to Moscow in 1923 for military training before returning to China to take charge of the Whampoa Military Academy, at which officers in the NRA were trained. At Whampoa, therefore, Chiang was able to create a core of young army officers who were loyal to him. On the death of Sun Yat-sen in 1925, Chiang's power base in the army helped him to secure the succession. He married Soong Mei Ling, the sister-in-law of Sun Yat-sen and the daughter of a wealthy Shanghai businessman. These connections, and his links to the Shanghai criminal underworld, helped him in his rise to power and his subsequent career. After the Communists took power in China in 1949, Chiang set up a nationalist government in Taiwan, where he was president until his death in 1975.

Nationalist rule

Over the course of the next 10 years, Chiang Kai-shek consolidated his control over China. Under the GMD, the country once again became ruled by a single central government, although in reality China remained a loose federation of semi independent provinces. The building of new roads, railways and airports improved internal communications and cities such as Shanghai became thriving industrial and commercial centres. Foreign influence, especially over trade and industry, remained strong but the Chinese government did regain control over the collection of customs duties. Politically, China was essentially a one-party State under Chiang's dictatorship. Chiang was both President and Commander-in-Chief of the army; he had close links to powerful banking and commercial interests, and he used an extensive secret police network to spy on and repress any opposition.

Communist survival

As Chiang's power grew, the CPC's own survival was severely threatened. Forced to abandon its city strongholds after the events of 1927, and with its membership plummeting, the Communists retreated to remote rural areas. Mao Zedong was forced to leave Hunan and establish a base in a mountainous area in Jiangxi province. Mao, who had always differed from the CPC leadership in advocating working with the peasants in rural areas rather than the official line of building up a membership among industrial workers in the cities, was well placed to take the lead in the new base area. By 1931, he had become Party Secretary and head of the government in the Jiangxi base area, now known as the **Chinese Soviet Republic**. By confiscating land from the landlords for redistribution to the poorer peasants and instituting reforms which improved the rights of women, Mao was able to win support and consolidate communist control over this region. Nevertheless, the position of the Communists in Jiangxi became increasingly precarious as Chiang's army made several attempts to crush this independent communist outpost. By 1934, the military situation had become so dangerous that a decision was made to abandon the Jiangxi base area and break out to find a more secure base elsewhere.

Chinese Soviet Republic: this term was borrowed from the Russian revolutionaries of 1917, who based their power on the Soviets – councils of workers', soldiers' and peasants' representatives. By using the term 'Soviet Republic', the Chinese Communists were consciously declaring the revolutionary nature of their regime.

The Long March

What followed was the Long March of 1934–5, which has been given legendary status by Communist Party propaganda ever since. Although recent studies have questioned the official CPC version of the events of the Long March, it is nevertheless true that the Communists, under Mao's leadership, broke out of the Jiangxi base area and headed west on foot. After several changes of direction, crossing 18 mountain ranges, fighting through the ranks of four GMD armies, 368 days and a journey of 12,500 km (7,700 miles) the survivors arrived in the area around Yan'an in Shaanxi province. Of the 80,000 who had originally set out, only about 5,000 survived the rigours of the journey and GMD attacks. The area in which they finally set up a new base was desolate and barren. By the mid-1930s, it seemed that the CPC was on the verge of extinction.

War against Japan

What completely transformed the situation in China was an external threat from Japan. Since the 1890s Japan, a growing power in the Far East, had been gaining territory from China. First the island of Taiwan and the Korean peninsula were taken by Japan in 1895. After the First World War, Japan was given control over former German concessions in China by Western powers, without any reference to the Chinese government. In 1931, Japan began a newly aggressive phase of expansion in China when Manchuria was occupied. With no outside help, and with his priority being to crush the Communists in China, Chiang Kai-shek put up little resistance to Japanese aggression. In the summer of 1937, however, the Japanese launched an even more serious threat to China when a Japanese army occupied Beijing, the beginning of a campaign to take control over the whole of northern China. At this point Chiang realised that if he did not resist, his own position would be threatened. He called a national conference to coordinate resistance, to which the Communists were invited. Mao declared that the Communists would support a policy of 'total resistance by the whole nation'. The United Front between Nationalists and Communists was, in theory at least, revived. The pressure on the CPC had been relieved and the Party was able to rebuild and expand.

Nationalist retreat

Over the next four years, the Japanese extended the area under their control southwards to the Yangzi River basin, including the city of Nanjing. They also captured Shanghai, Guangzhou and Hong Kong so that, by the end of 1941, they were in control of most of the Chinese coastline. Chiang was forced to retreat and move his capital city to Chongqing in the south. He now controlled only central southern and western China, and even in these areas his control was not total. Meanwhile, the Communists had begun to revive. Outside Yan'an there were still remnants of the CPC in the old base area of Jiangxi. In Yan'an, Mao established himself for the first time as the undisputed leader of the CPC through the Yan'an Rectification campaign of 1942. With a more open recruitment policy, Party membership began to grow; from 40,000 members in 1937, the CPC had grown to 800,000 by 1940. The communist armies showed similar increases in size. By implementing policies of rent control, and campaigns to improve literacy and stamp out corruption among officials, the CPC gradually began win over the support of the peasants. Above all, the Communists were seen to be achieving some military successes against the Japanese,

Cross-reference

See page 38 for more on the **Yan'an Rectification campaign**.

in contrast to Chiang and the GMD whose military campaigns mostly ended in defeat. Mao adopted **guerrilla warfare** tactics which tied down large numbers of Japanese troops and won the Communists respect from other Chinese people.

By the late 1930s, communist forces in China were showing signs of a revival in their fortunes after appearing to be on the verge of extinction in 1935. As long as the war against Japan continued, however, the struggle for control of China would have to be postponed.

Key term

Guerrilla warfare: the key features of guerrilla warfare are to divide an army into small, lightly armed, mobile bands which can merge into the civilian population and attack the larger enemy forces at their weakest points. Key targets for guerrilla bands would be the enemy's lines of communication and supply. A key principle of guerrilla warfare according to Mao was to retreat when the enemy concentrates a vastly superior force but to attack when and where the enemy least expects it.

Timeline

The colours represent events relating to China during the period: Black: Political, Red: Economic, Blue: Social, Green: International/China's place in the world

1893	1900	1911	1912	1917	1919	1921	1927
Mao Zedong is born in Hunan province	Boxer Rising against growing foreign influence in China	Revolution in China	Abdication of the last Qing emperor and proclamation of the Chinese Republic	China enters the First World War on the side of Britain, France, the USA and Russia	May 4th Movement student protests against Allies' decision to hand over former German possessions in China to Japan	Communist Party of China (CPC) is established	Massacre of Communists by nationalist forces in Shanghai

1945	1945	1946	1946	1948	1949	1949	1950	1950
Mao flies to meet Chiang Kai-shek for peace talks under American auspices	**October** Mao and Chiang reach agreement on the principles of a peace deal but fighting between Communists and Nationalists intensifies	**January** The USA persuades both sides to agree a ceasefire	**July** The ceasefire breaks down and Civil War begins	**November** Communist forces capture Manchuria	**January** Communist forces capture Beijing	**October** Communists defeat Nationalists and establish the People's Republic of China (PRC)	Start of the Korean War	New Marriage Law gives more legal protection to women

1957	1958	1959	1962	1962	1962	1963	1964	1966
The Hundred Flowers campaign encourages intellectuals to criticise the Party, followed by the anti-Rightist purge of intellectuals	Mao launches the Great Leap Forward (Second Five Year Plan for industry)	Purge of Peng Dehuai from the Party leadership	Launch of the Third Five Year Plan for industry	Start of a power struggle between Mao and Liu Shaoqi/ Deng Xiaoping	Launch of the *Little Red Book* of quotations by Chairman Mao	Launch of the Socialist Education Movement to spread Mao's ideas and purge the Party	China successfully tests its first atomic bomb	Mao launches the Cultural Revolution

1931	1931	1934–5	1937	1937	1941	1941	1945	1945
Communist base area is established in Jiangxi province but under severe military pressure from Nationalists	Japanese invasion of Manchuria	The Long March: Mao leads communist forces in a break out from Jiangxi on a 12,500 km trek to Yan'an	Japanese forces occupy Beijing and begin a campaign to occupy the rest of China	Communists and Nationalists form a United Front against Japanese invaders	Nationalist forces attack Communists in the south of China	The USA enters the Second World War against Japan after the attack on Pearl Harbur	**August** The Japanese surrender after atomic bomb attacks on Hiroshima and Nagasaki	Soviet troops occupy Manchuria

1950	1951	1952	1952	1953	1953	1953	1955
Suppression of Counter-revolutionaries campaign begins	Three-Antis campaign begins to eradicate corruption among Party and government officials	Five-Antis campaign is launched to eradicate corruption among businessmen	First Agricultural Producers' Cooperatives are established	End of the Korean War	Launch of the First Five Year Plan for industry	Purge of Gao Gang and Rao Shushi from the Party leadership	'Higher-stage' Agricultural Producers' Cooperatives mark a decisive shift towards the collectivisation of agriculture

1967	1969	1971	1972	1973	1976	1976	1976
The January Revolution in Shanghai results in the overthrow of Party leadership in the city by Red Guards. This is followed by the February Crackdown in which the People's Liberation Army starts to suppress Red Guard violence	The Cultural Revolution is officially declared to be over by Party Congress	Lin Biao dies in an air crash after an unsuccessful attempt at a coup	American president Richard Nixon visits China to begin the process of restoring normal relations between the two powers	Anti-Confucius campaign is launched by the Gang of Four	**January** Death of Zhou Enlai	**April** Demonstrations against the Gang of Four in Tiananmen Square	**September** Mao dies

1 Communists and Nationalists

In this chapter you will learn about:

- why the Civil War broke out in China in 1946
- what happened during the Civil War.

Fig. 1 *Guomindang soldiers surrender to communist forces during the Civil War*

Fig. 2 *The situation in China at the end of the Second World War*

China is a vast country riven by major cultural and ethnic divisions. The challenge facing both Chiang Kai-shek and Mao Zedong was how to unite this huge territory under their own political system. The struggle to do so would create one of the bloodiest civil wars in history.

■ Long-term causes of the Civil War

Conflict between Nationalists and Communists

Fig. 3 *Dead and wounded Chinese lie in the street after fighting between Guomindang and communist forces in Guangzhou, 1927*

The Chinese Civil War, which began in 1946 as a struggle for control of China, had its roots in the conflict between Communists and Nationalists that had begun in 1927. Throughout the years 1927–37, the nationalist government of Chiang Kai-shek had tried to eradicate the Communist Party and impose one-party rule on the whole of China. By 1937, after the episode of the Long March, the Communists were confined largely to the area around Yan'an. The Japanese invasion of parts of China in 1937 led to a temporary cessation of hostilities between the Nationalists and the Communists, who formed a United Front against the invaders. Chiang Kai-shek, however, was still unwilling to accept the Communists as partners in the struggle against the Japanese. In 1941, Chiang's NRA forces launched an attack against communist forces in the south of China, thereby breaching the United Front. Despite this being a military setback for the Communists, politically they gained from this incident. Their propaganda was able to portray Chiang as being more interested in fighting his fellow Chinese and thus dividing the nation, whereas the Communists were able to present themselves as the true Chinese patriots in concentrating on the fight against the Japanese. The stage was set for a full-scale renewal of hostilities between the two forces once the war against Japan was over.

The Second World War in the Far East

For China, the war against Japan began in 1937. For Western powers that had military bases, colonial possessions and economic interests in the Far East, the war began in December 1941 when the Japanese navy launched a surprise attack on the American fleet at Pearl Harbor in Hawaii. British bases in Singapore and Hong Kong were attacked and captured soon after.

■ Cross-reference

The **conflict between the Nationalists and the Communists** after Chiang Kai-shek's forces had massacred the Communists in Shanghai in 1927, are dealt with in more detail on pages 4–7.

Fig. 4 *The Guomindang leader, Chiang Kai-shek, with his wife*

The entry of the USA and Britain into the war in the Far East in December 1941 provided Chiang's government with much needed foreign allies. The Americans began to supply Chiang's armies with weapons and ammunition, and built airbases on Chinese soil which were used to launch bombing raids on Japan itself. In response, the Japanese started the Ichigo offensive in April 1944, which was aimed at capturing the American bases. This was the first major Japanese ground offensive against nationalist forces in China since 1938. Many of the Chinese forces gave up their positions without a fight, exposing serious problems within the nationalist armies. Morale was low because troops were unpaid, unfed and unfit, and lacked basic training and equipment. Corrupt officers stole money which was intended for pay and supplies. Chiang did not trust his generals and was constantly interfering in their decisions, even though he was far removed from the action. The result was a major defeat for the nationalist forces and a serious blow to Chiang's prestige.

The end of the war

The Second World War in the Far East ended in August 1945 with the surrender of Japanese forces to the Allies after the dropping of atomic bombs on Hiroshima and Nagasaki. At the end of the war, Chiang Kai-shek's government in Chongqing was still recognised by foreign powers as the legitimate government of China. The Communists had strengthened their position in Yan'an and had impressed many nationalist-minded Chinese with their energy, determination and discipline in the fight against the Japanese. Given the legacy of nearly 20 years of conflict between the GMD and the CPC, it was likely that the internal struggle would continue once the war was over. In this renewed conflict, however, the odds were stacked heavily in favour of Chiang Kai-shek and his government.

■ Short-term causes of the Civil War

A divided country

At the end of the war China was once again a divided country. Although Chiang Kai-shek's nationalist government claimed to be the government of the whole of China, it actually controlled only a fraction of the country's territory. As Figure 2 on page 10 shows, the main territorial divisions in China in August 1945 were:

■ Japanese forces still occupied the north of China, much of the Chinese coastline and most of the large cities.

■ The Nationalists (Guomindang) controlled a large area of southern and central China from their capital city in Chongqing.

■ The Communists (CPC) controlled much of the countryside in northern and north-eastern China from their base in Yan'an.

■ The Soviet Union's **Red Army** had moved into Manchuria on 8 August 1945.

At the time of the Japanese surrender, Nationalists and Communists tried to occupy as much territory as possible. Both sides were trying to strengthen their position. At this stage, however, the Nationalists had a distinct advantage. Chiang Kai-shek's government was recognised by foreign powers as the legitimate government of China and was therefore given the right to take the surrender of Japanese forces still based in China. American aircraft airlifted 100,000 nationalist troops to the north so that they could do this, but in doing so they were moving into areas that were under communist control. In response, the Communists began to move into Manchuria, where they received from the Red Army many of the weapons and ammunition captured from the Japanese. There were clashes between communist and nationalist troops in many parts of China.

A legacy of conflict

Years of conflict and rivalry between Nationalists and Communists had left a legacy of mistrust and suspicion. It seemed to many observers at the time that Civil War in China was unavoidable. The aims of the two parties were very different. The Guomindang had close links with business interests and landlords and was in favour of maintaining a capitalist, private enterprise system in China. The Communists aimed for a revolutionary overthrow of the regime followed by the confiscation of large estates from the landlords and of businesses from their private owners. This would prepare the way for a more equal, classless society in which the ownership of land and business would be shared by all. For the Communists, however, these were long-term aims. Few Communists believed that a communist revolution in China was a realistic possibility in the near future. In the short term their aim was to consolidate their position in the areas under their control and to take what opportunities they might find to extend their influence. For tactical reasons, Mao had been prepared to cooperate with the Guomindang in the past and there was a possibility that such cooperation might continue in the future.

Attempts to find a peaceful solution

Both the USA and the Soviet Union wished to avoid a civil war in China so soon after the Second World War. Under American pressure, therefore, Chiang Kai-shek agreed to peace talks with the Communists. On 28 August 1945, the American ambassador to China, Patrick Hurley, personally escorted Mao Zedong to Chongqing for talks with Chiang Kai-shek. Although a ceasefire was supposed to be in operation while the talks progressed, fighting continued in some parts of the country. By October 1945 an agreement was reached in which both sides committed in principle to:

■ a democratic political system, with free elections and guarantees of personal freedoms

■ a unified military force (i.e. a continuation of the wartime United Front)

■ elections for a **national assembly**.

Agreement on these broad, general principles was relatively easy to achieve; much more difficult to resolve were the details over who should control the military forces and local governments in areas under communist control. Mao was not prepared to relinquish communist control on the ground whereas Chiang was determined to extend nationalist control over the whole of the country. Almost immediately after the agreement was signed, therefore, fighting intensified when Chiang sent his forces north into Manchuria. The communist position was severely weakened when Stalin, the Russian leader, ordered the Communists to hand over the cities in Manchuria to the Nationalists.

Activity

Thinking point

Given the ideological differences between the Nationalists and the Communists, and the long history of conflict between the two, was there any realistic prospect of peaceful cooperation between them after the end of the Second World War?

Key term

National assembly: a parliament for the whole of China, based on a democratic franchise.

Fig. 5 *Mao Zedong (centre) about to board his plane taking him back to Yan'an in October 1945, after peace talks in Chongqing with Chiang Kai-shek*

Exploring the detail

Democratic political systems

A democratic system is one in which power is vested in the people. In practice, this usually means a system in which people have a free vote to choose representatives for a parliament (national assembly), which then has the authority to make laws. In a democratic system, essential personal freedoms, such as the right to free speech, a free press, the freedom to practice a religion and the freedom to set up political parties, are guaranteed by law.

The start of the Civil War

In December 1945, President Truman of the USA sent General George Marshall to China as his envoy on a mission to mediate between the two sides in the conflict. Marshall succeeded in persuading both sides to agree to a ceasefire in January 1946 and pressured Chiang into calling a political conference to discuss the future government of China. The conference, with representatives from all of China's main political parties, succeeded in reaching an outline agreement on a constitution. Once again, however, the agreement fell apart almost as soon as it was signed. When the Guomindang tried to make crucial changes to the terms of the agreement, which would have created an autocratic form of government headed by them, the Communists and other parties withdrew their cooperation. The Nationalists went ahead anyway and drafted a new constitution without the participation of other parties. Marshall made another attempt to mediate by arranging a ceasefire in Manchuria in June 1946, but even as he did so the Guomindang forces were preparing for a major offensive against communist forces in Manchuria, which began in July. At the same time, the Communists seized the key industrial city of Harbin in northern Manchuria and consolidated their control over rural areas. By the late summer of 1946, an all-out civil war had begun in China. The USA's attempts at mediation had failed and Marshall returned home in January 1947.

Key profile

General George Marshall

George Marshall (1880–1959) had supervised the US army and been chief military adviser to President Roosevelt during the Second World War and was described by Churchill as the 'architect of victory'. In December 1945, President Truman sent Marshall to China to mediate between the Nationalists and Communists and to try to persuade both sides to set up a coalition government. His mission was a failure.

A closer look

Mao's attitude towards peace negotiations

Just before Mao went to Chongqing at the end of August 1945 for peace talks with the Guomindang leader Chiang Kai-shek, he outlined his views on the situation in two important documents. The first of these, 'A Declaration on the Current Situation' was a public document issued on 25 August. The following day, Mao issued another document, 'On Peace Negotiations with the Guomindang', which was intended for the eyes of Communist Party members only. Source 1 is adapted from the first, public document.

After the surrender of Japanese imperialism, the important task confronting the whole nation is to consolidate unity in the country, safeguard domestic peace, bring about democracy and improve the people's livelihood so as, on the basis of peace, democracy and unity, to achieve national unification and build a new China, independent, free, prosperous and powerful.

| 1 | *Chairman Mao, 25 August 1945. From **Selected Works of Mao Tse-tung*** |

Source 2 is adapted from the document issued to Party members only.

The speedy surrender of the Japanese forces has changed the whole situation. Chiang Kai-shek has monopolised the right to accept the surrender, and for the time being the big cities and important lines of communication will not be in our hands. Nevertheless, in northern China we should still fight hard, fight with all our might to take all we can. In the past two weeks our army has recovered 59 cities of various sizes and vast rural areas, thus winning a great victory. In the coming period we should continue the offensive. We should gain control of whatever we can, even though temporarily.

| 2 | *Chairman Mao, 26 August 1945. From **Selected Works of Mao Tse-tung*** |

Source 3 is also adapted from the document issued to Party members only.

It is possible that after the negotiations the Guomindang may conditionally recognise our Party's status. Our Party too may conditionally recognise the status of the Guomindang. This would bring about a new stage of cooperation between the two parties and of peaceful development. We on our side are prepared to make such concessions as are necessary and as do not damage the fundamental interests of the people. Without such concessions we cannot expose the Guomindang's civil war plot, cannot gain the political initiative, cannot win the sympathy of world public opinion and cannot obtain in exchange legal status for our Party and a state of peace. But there are limits to such concessions; the principle is that they must not damage the fundamental interests of the people.

| 3 | *Chairman Mao, 26 August 1945. From **Selected Works of Mao Tse-tung*** |

Activity

Source analysis

Study Sources 1, 2 and 3. These sources express Mao's views on the situation facing the Communist Party in August 1945.

1. Explain how far Source 2 differs from Source 1 in relation to Mao's approach to the peace talks with the Guomindang.

2. The following list contains possible explanations for the differences between Sources 1 and 2. Consider each point in turn and explain why you do or do not accept this explanation.

   - Mao was indecisive; he could not decide what to do.

   - Mao was being devious, saying different things to different audiences.

   - Mao was keeping his options open so that he could decide on his policy as the situation developed.

3. In what ways does Source 3 help to explain more fully Mao's attitude towards the peace talks with the Guomindang?

Mao Zedong and the events of the Civil War

Fig. 6 *Mao Zedong (right) attends a military strategy conference in December 1946*

Phases of the Civil War

Phase 1: early setbacks, July 1946 to May 1947

In the first months of the Civil War the Guomindang, with a larger army and better equipment, took the initiative and forced the Communists on to the defensive. The Guomindang offensive, which began in July 1946, succeeded in capturing control of the large cities and establishing a GMD-controlled 'corridor' along the coast of Manchuria from Jinzhou to Shenyang and on to Changchun. Communist forces in Manchuria were forced to retreat northwards across the Sungari River. Elsewhere in China the Communists were also in retreat. They lost control of their former base in Yan'an from which Lin Biao, one of Mao's most senior and trusted military commanders, had already moved the Communist **Eighth Route Army** northwards to Manchuria in order to strengthen Communist forces there.

Further south in China there were more reverses for the Communists. They were forced to abandon their isolated positions in the eastern Yangzi River area and, in October, they lost their last remaining city stronghold outside Manchuria at Zhangjiakou. Manchuria was the key battleground in the early stages of the war. Chiang committed over half a million of his best troops to the capture of the region. In October 1946, a renewed offensive by GMD forces against the Communist stronghold of northern Manchuria failed to break the People's Liberation Army (PLA) defences.

From their rural base the Communists adopted an effective guerrilla warfare strategy against the GMD. By ambushing GMD units that ventured outside the cities and blowing up the railway lines on which the GMD's city-based forces depended for their supplies and reinforcements, the PLA and local communist militia forces were able to isolate the

Key term

Eighth Route Army: in 1937, the Communists' Red Army in Yan'an was renamed the Eighth Route Army. In line with the policy of establishing a United Front with the Guomindang, it was placed under the overall command of the Guomindang. At the same time, the remnants of communist guerrilla forces in central China, who had been left behind at the time of the Long March, were reorganised into the Fourth Route Army. Both armies were actually controlled by veteran communist officers who conducted effective guerrilla campaigns against the Japanese.

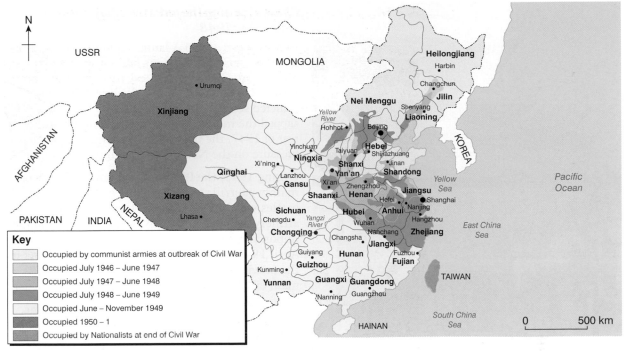

Fig. 7 *The communist takeover of China, 1946–51*

Nationalists' city strongholds. By the spring of 1947, the Communists' control over northern Manchuria was virtually unshakeable and Lin Biao decided to move on to an offensive strategy.

> The military attaché and I approached Tsinan – the capital of Shandong province – flying low over the Tsin-Pu railroad to see how much damage had been done by the Communists. Their guerrilla activities have been especially successful in disrupting railroads, which are essential for the more conventional type of warfare practised by the Nationalists but have little relevance for Communist tactics. The Nationalists have yet to learn this lesson and act accordingly. Although there has been more reconstruction than we had expected, there are long stretches between Taian and Tsinan where even the embankments have vanished.

4
An American observer reports on the war, 1947
*From J. F. Melby, **The Mandate of Heaven**, 1968*

Key profile

Lin Biao

Lin Biao (1908–71) was the son of a landlord from Hubei province. He graduated from the Whampoa Military Academy in 1925 and quickly established himself as one of the Communist Party's most able military commanders. His talents as a guerrilla leader were put to the test in the Communists' struggle for survival in Jiangxi in the early 1930s and later in Yan'an. During the Civil War, he was the PLA commander in Manchuria and, later, in northern China. He successfully transformed the PLA from a guerrilla force into a modern professional army.

Activity

Thinking point

Using the information in this section, explain why Manchuria was the key battleground in the early stages of the war. You may find it helpful to organise your thoughts under three main headings:

- geographical location
- economic importance
- strategic importance.

Exploring the detail

The start of the Civil War

The Guomindang offensive against communist forces in Manchuria, which began in July 1946, is usually taken to be the start of a full-scale civil war in China. This was not the end, however, of American efforts to bring the two sides together and broker a ceasefire. George Marshall remained in China until January 1947 but President Truman was finally forced to abandon American peacemaking efforts when it became clear that neither side was prepared to be flexible.

Fig. 8 *After the PLA's victory in Manchuria in autumn 1948, PLA forces began to move south into northern China. In this photograph, a PLA force is seen marching through the Great Wall at Shanhaiguan*

Phase 2: seizing the initiative, May 1947 to November 1948

In May 1947, the PLA launched full-scale assaults on GMD positions but, without an air force to provide support, these first attacks were unsuccessful. Nevertheless, the heavy fighting inflicted serious losses on the GMD forces and sapped the morale of its troops. Throughout the rest of 1947, the Communists maintained their pressure on the Nationalists using guerrilla attacks.

During 1948, the PLA moved from a strategy of mainly guerrilla warfare to one of conventional battles with massed forces of infantry and artillery. In northern China the PLA captured the important city of Luoyang on the Yellow River in April 1948 and began to make significant gains in the province of Shandong, isolating the GMD's main city stronghold of Jinan.

In June 1948, the Communists captured Kaifeng, also on the Yellow River. As the Yellow River valley was a crucial means of access from the coast into the western interior of China, gaining control over these cities meant that the Communists could begin to threaten nationalist control over Xian and Sichuan in the west. The city of Jinan (Shandong province) was captured in September 1948.

There were a series of spectacular communist victories in Manchuria in October and November. On 15 October, the PLA captured the key railway junction at Jinzhou, in many ways the gateway to Manchuria from the rest of China. With Jinzhou in communist hands, the nationalist forces in Manchuria were now trapped and the PLA was able to pick them off one at a time. The capture of Changchun in October was followed by the fall of Shenyang on 2 November. The loss of Manchuria was a body blow to the Nationalists; over 400,000 troops were lost while the damage to GMD morale was incalculable.

■ Exploring the detail

Conventional warfare

Modern armies are normally organised and equipped to fight large set-piece battles in which artillery weapons and aircraft are used to bombard the enemy's defences before the main attack begins. The attack by ground forces (infantry, tanks and motorised units) is then launched to capture the enemy's positions and so take control of an area.

■ Activity

Talking point

Discuss why it was important for the Communists' chances of winning the war to switch from a strategy of guerrilla warfare to one of conventional warfare.

2 November 1948. Shenyang surrendered yesterday and that, I guess, is that. All that is needed now is a few mopping up operations and the sweep to the Yangzi will be complete. Nothing can save Beijing and Tientsin because there is nothing left with which to defend them.

1 December 1948. Hsuchow fell today at the end of the biggest pitched battle of the war. Now only Fu Zuoyi [nationalist commander] holds out between Siberia and the Yangzi, and if he holds out or even puts up a fight instead of arranging a deal, it will only prove there is something new under the sun. Nanjing begins to look like a city that was, and night after night the trucks rumble down to the barges on the river as the government continues its move to the south. It is done at night to avoid any possibility of a communist attack by day on the shipping going downstream.

5

A diary of life during the Civil War.
From J. F. Melby, **The Mandate of Heaven,** *1968*

Phase 3: the final stages, December 1948 to October 1949

Moving quickly to capitalise on its successes in Manchuria and Shandong, the PLA launched two new offensives in northern China. The first against the vital railway junction of Xuzhou resulted in a battle lasting 65 days in December 1948 and January 1949. With 600,000 troops on each side committed to this battle, both sides recognised its military and its psychological importance. This defeat of the Nationalists was yet another major blow.

The second offensive was directed against Beijing, the old imperial capital. Lin Biao and the PLA moved first against Tianjin to the south of Beijing in January 1949, thereby effectively cutting off Beijing from the rest of China. Beijing itself was captured with little resistance on 31 January. The whole of northern China, including Manchuria, was now under communist control.

In the spring of 1949 there was a lull in the fighting. The PLA rested its troops while consolidating its position in China north of the Yangzi River. A communist-led provisional people's government was set up in northern China.

In April, the PLA returned to the offensive by attacking key cities on the Yangzi River. Nanjing, which had been the nationalist stronghold and capital city of China since 1927, was captured on 23 April and Shanghai, the commercial capital of China, fell to the Communists in late May. The way to the south was now open.

After the capture of Wuhan in May, the PLA forces were divided for the final assault on GMD territory. One force, led by Peng Dehuai, struck westwards from Wuhan towards Xi'an and Lanzhou, both of which were taken in August 1949. Another PLA force led by Lin Biao marched south towards Guangzhou (Canton) which was captured in October, while part of Lin Biao's force was sent south-westwards to mop up the remaining GMD resistance in Guizhou and Chongqing, both of which were taken in November.

> ### ■ Exploring the detail
>
> #### Stalin's concerns
>
> In early spring 1949, the Soviet leader Joseph Stalin attempted to persuade Mao to stop the offensive against nationalist forces in the south and establish a communist regime only in the north of China. Stalin was concerned that the Americans might intervene if they believed that Chiang Kai-shek's regime was on the point of final collapse. Mao ignored Stalin's concerns and pushed on to final victory in the whole of China.

Fig. 9 *PLA forces march into Nanjing in April 1949*

Key terms

Politburo: short for political bureau. This group of 14 senior members of the Party, elected by the larger Central Committee, was the Party's major decision-making body. In practice, the smaller Standing Committee of the Politburo made most of the day-to-day decisions.

People's Republic of China (PRC): on 1 October 1949, Mao proclaimed the founding of the People's Republic of China.

Key profile

Peng Dehuai

Peng Dehuai (1898–1974) was a veteran of the Communist Party's struggles during the 1930s, particularly the Long March., and had been a communist commander during the Second World War. He joined the Party **Politburo** in 1945. After 1954 Peng Dehuai became Defence Minister and Commander-in-Chief of the PLA, following his successful command over the Chinese forces during the Korean War (1950–3).

By late September, with most of China under communist control, Mao called a Political Consultative Conference in Beijing. Although dominated by the Communists, there were representatives from 14 other parties at the conference. This conference elected the members of the new central government of the **People's Republic of China (PRC)**, including Mao Zedong as its Chairman. Desperate to avoid capture by the Communists, Chiang Kai-shek fled to the island of Taiwan and established a Guomindang government there.

Activity

Revision exercise

Copy and complete the table below. In the second column list the main battles/events of each phase of the Civil War. In the last column, select one key event for each phase that marked an important turning point in the war and write a short explanation to show why it was important.

	Major events of each phase of the Civil War	Key turning points and their importance
Phase 1		
Phase 2		
Phase 3		

Summary questions

1. Explain why civil war was likely by August 1945.
2. Explain why civil war broke out in 1946.

2 War and communist victory

I missed the first contingents of infantry and cavalry, as well as part of the motorised units. But in what I did see, lasting about an hour, I counted over 250 heavy motor vehicles of all kinds – tanks, armoured cars, trucks of soldiers, trucks mounted with machine-guns, trucks towing heavy artillery. Behind them followed innumerable ambulances, jeeps and other smaller vehicles. As probably the greatest demonstration of military might in history, the spectacle was enormously impressive. But what made it especially memorable to Americans was the fact that it was primarily a display of American military equipment, virtually all of it captured or obtained by bribe from Guomindang forces in the short space of two and a half years.

1

An American observer reports on the PLA's march into Beijing, February 1949

The political and military strength of the Communist Party in 1946

Table 1 *Estimated strength of nationalist and communist forces in China, August 1945*

	Nationalists	Communists
Troops	2,800,000	320,000
Artillery pieces	6,000	600

Note: These figures are estimates. Other sources give estimates of communist strength at around 800,000 to 900,000 troops in 1945. However, all sources agree that the Communists had far fewer troops than the Nationalists.

*Source: J. D. Spence, **The Search for Modern China**, 1990*

Table 1 shows that, at the end of the Second World War, the nationalist forces in China had an overwhelming advantage over the Communists in both numbers of troops and equipment. You should note also that the Nationalists had an air force with aircraft supplied by their American allies whereas the Communists had no aircraft. The communist forces were concentrated in 19 base areas including their main base in Yan'an; over the country as a whole the CPC ruled over some 90 million people in a country of about 600 million. During the course of 1945 and early 1946, nationalist forces drove the Communists out of most of their base areas. From a military point of view, therefore, it appeared that the Nationalists had the best chance of winning the Civil War. There were, however, a number of political and military factors that strengthened the Communists' position.

Fig. 1 *Mao Zedong (left) and other leading communists at the Seventh Party Congress of the CPC in 1945*

Political unity

In its first 20 years, the Communist Party of China had been split by disputes between rival factions. By 1945, this was in the past. During the period the Communists spent in Yan'an, Mao established himself as the undisputed leader of the Party, either by outwitting and removing his opponents or by winning the arguments. His leadership was authoritarian and he was determined to ensure that his political line – Mao Zedong Thought – was accepted and followed by the rest of the Party. Debates over policy and strategy were allowed within the top Party leadership but these no longer became the focus for bitter divisions within the Party. Mao's reputation had been established during the Yan'an years because his policy of building a party based on the peasants and his strategy of fighting a guerrilla war had been proved to be the most practical strategy to follow.

Party unity was the foundation on which communist success was built. It gave the leadership of the Communist Party, including the top-ranking political and military leaders, an aura of confidence and authority. This impressed not only lower-ranking Communists but also people who were not members of the Party.

Democratic dictatorship

In areas under communist control – the so-called 'liberated areas' – Mao imposed a form of government that combined elements of dictatorship with elements of democracy. All political activity and decision making was under the leadership and guidance of the Communist Party, but at a local level there was scope for non-members from among the peasants and other classes to participate in 'revolutionary committees' and mass meetings. These committees dealt with education, health, farming and land reform as well as political and military training. This mass participation was an important factor in building up support for communist rule in these areas. The system of local government established by the Communists in rural areas was the first effective local administration these areas had ever experienced.

Experience on the battlefield

Communist forces had developed their skills of fighting a guerrilla war during the long struggle against the Japanese. These skills would be of great value in the coming Civil War against the Nationalists. The communist forces did not, however, have experience of fighting conventional battles, which would prove to be a disadvantage in the early stages of the war.

Motivation

Mao firmly believed that a successful army needed troops who were motivated by an ideological commitment to the struggle. Political indoctrination of communist troops, therefore, was a vital part of their training. Not only would this mean that communist forces would endure the dangers and sacrifices of a long and hard military campaign better than their less committed opponents, but they would also be a vital means by which communist propaganda was spread. When communist troops entered an area not previously under their control, they would be the first Communists the local inhabitants would encounter. They had an important role in winning over the local population to the communist cause.

The strengths and weaknesses of the Guomindang in 1946

Military

As Table 1 on page 21 shows, the Guomindang possessed an army that was far larger and better equipped than the communist forces at the beginning of the Civil War. They also had an air force that could provide

their troops on the ground with aerial support, something that military strategists believed was crucial in modern warfare. Although nationalist forces had not achieved much success in the war against Japan, they had gained experience of fighting conventional battles which communist forces were lacking.

On the other hand, many nationalist troops were poorly trained, low on morale and lacking in discipline. When taking over areas formerly controlled by Communists, nationalist troops gained a reputation for brutality and ill-discipline among local populations who were often terrorised into submission. This was a mainly conscript army in which ordinary soldiers had little

Fig. 2 *Mao Zedong talks to soldiers of the PLA*

incentive to fight. Troops often went days without food and water and their pay was frequently stolen by their officers. Heavy losses in battle and desertions severely weakened the nationalist armies.

> There is good evidence that apathy, resentment and defeatism are spreading fast in nationalist ranks, causing surrenders and desertions. Main factors contributing to this are: Communists ever mounting numerical superiority; nationalist soldiers' discouragement over prospects of getting reinforcements; better solidarity and fighting spirit of Communists; losses and exhaustion of Nationalists.

 2

Adapted from a report from an American consul in Shenyang, May 1947

Territorial control

Territorially, the Nationalists controlled more territory than the Communists. Not only did the GMD have, in theory at least, most of the Chinese population under their rule, they also crucially controlled most of China's large cities, most of the railway network and most of the main waterways.

Nationalist 'control' in many areas, however, was never complete. Many warlords had not been defeated by the Guomindang. Instead, compromises had been reached that left warlords in control over their own areas while the Nationalists were in charge of the central government. Lack of effective control over the whole country weakened the ability of the Nationalists to mobilise the whole nation in support of their struggle.

Foreign support

Foreign support was a major asset to the Nationalists. The Guomindang government was recognised by foreign powers, including the Soviet Union, as the legitimate government of China. The Americans supplied military equipment to the Nationalists and American transport aircraft airlifted nationalist troops to the north in August 1945 so that they could be in position to accept the Japanese surrender.

Foreign support, however, came at a cost to the Nationalists. Chiang Kai-shek's dependence on foreign aid undermined his claim to be the true defender of the nation's interests. At the same time, Chiang's allies grew increasingly critical of his style of government and his personal failings. The Americans' frustration with Chiang is well reflected in the comment by the American general Joseph Stilwell, who was sent to China during the Second World War to liaise with the Nationalists. 'Chiang same as ever,' he wrote, 'a grasping, bigoted, ungrateful little rattlesnake.'

■ Key profile

Joseph Stilwell

Joseph Stilwell (1883–1946) was the American military commander in the China–Burma–India theatre of operations during the Second World War. As such, he was the American officer who had the responsibility for liaising with the leader of the nationalist Chinese government, Chiang Kai-shek. Stilwell's clashes with Chiang caused him to be replaced in 1944 by another American general. He gained the nickname 'Vinegar Joe' because of his reputation for being difficult to work with and his sharp tongue.

Lack of popular support

The Guomindang's three principles – Nationalism, democracy, people's livelihood – had attracted widespread support for the Party in the 1920s and 1930s among China's educated middle classes. The failure of the nationalist government to deliver on any of these promises had seen much of this support ebb away. The party had failed to defend national interests; had created a dictatorial, not a democratic, regime; and had done little to improve the livelihood of the people. The Guomindang as a party stood aloof from society and had not tried to build mass support. Instead, Chiang's regime depended for its survival on the financial backing of wealthy businessmen and landlords and on the ruthlessness of the secret police in removing political opposition. Assassinations of political opponents, and the torture and execution of suspected Communists without trial, were all used to maintain Chiang's one-party State.

Corruption and inefficiency

The Guomindang regime was both corrupt and inefficient. Local officials abused their powers to enrich themselves by taking bribes and extorting money from local people. Taxes that should have been used to pay for the costs of administration and the armies were not collected in a fair and efficient way and much of the tax revenue failed to reach central government. The result was that Chiang's government was forced to borrow heavily and was permanently in debt.

Corruption was so widespread that the Guomindang set up a special organisation to combat it. It was the 'Tiger-Beating Squad' because people compared corrupt officials to fearsome tigers, and it invited people to send in their complaints. But it soon became apparent that this was a means for the really powerful to extort money from the rich. 'Tiger-Beating' was a lucrative job.

3   *Jung Chang, **Wild Swans**, 1992*

Chiang's leadership

As President of the Republic of China and leader of the Guomindang Party, Chiang Kai-shek was primarily responsible for the failures of his government:

- His regime was weak and divided by factional rivalry.
- He was hard-working and ruthless but he could not delegate power to his subordinates. He tried to control what his commanders on the battlefield were doing even though he was far removed from the action. Often his decisions were impractical and contradictory.
- He was a poor judge of character. He trusted those people whom he liked, even when it became apparent that some of them were incompetent or, even worse, working against him.
- He had a close network of supporters in the nationalist army and in business circles whom he rewarded with jobs and contracts. On the other hand, he was suspicious of more independent-minded men, especially among his commanders. Promotion and advancement in the nationalist army depended not on ability but on loyalty and connections.
- He did not act decisively to stamp out corruption or to remove incompetent officials.

Fig. 3 *Chiang Kai-shek's weaknesses*

Chiang's American allies had noted his weaknesses as a political leader and military commander during the Second World War. They had also commented on his stubbornness and inability to change. In the fast-moving events of the Civil War that was about to begin, Chiang's inflexible and dictatorial nature were serious disadvantages. Many of the serious strategic mistakes that were made by the nationalist forces were the result of decisions made by Chiang Kai-shek alone.

■ The impact on the people of communist discipline and land reforms

In an overwhelmingly rural society such as China in the 1940s, the support of the peasants was crucial to the success of any political party. Ever since the CPC had been driven out of major cities like Shanghai in 1927, it had concentrated on building up support with China's millions of peasants, particularly among the poorest peasants who Mao believed were the most revolutionary. Mao's strategy for winning peasant support had two main elements: discipline and land reforms.

Activity

Revision exercise

1 Summarise the main weaknesses of the Nationalists in the Civil War under the following headings: Political weaknesses; Military weaknesses.

2 Compare the leadership of Chairman Mao with that of Chiang Kai-shek. What were Mao's main strengths in comparison to Chiang?

Exploring the detail

The People's Liberation Army

Communist forces in the 1930s had generally been referred to as the Red Army, although in practice there were a number of separate forces (field armies) in different parts of China. In 1946, the various armies were reorganised into the People's Liberation Army, with a single command structure. The choice of the name reflected the Communists' term for the Civil War: the 'war of liberation'.

Disciplined behaviour by communist troops

Since 1928, Mao had impressed on soldiers in the communist forces the need for proper discipline and to treat the civilian population with respect. These rules were added to over the years and were then reissued to the army, now known as the People's Liberation Army (PLA) from 1946.

Three main rules of discipline:

1 Obey orders in all your actions.
2 Don't take a single needle or piece of thread from the masses.
3 Turn in everything captured.

Eight points for attention:

1 Speak politely.
2 Pay fairly for what you buy.
3 Return everything you borrow.
4 Pay for anything you damage.
5 Don't hit or swear at people.
6 Don't damage crops.
7 Don't take liberties with women.
8 Don't ill-treat captives.

4 *Instructions from the general headquarters of the PLA, 1947. From Selected Works of Mao Tse-tung*

Fig. 4 *Mao Zedong in northern Shaanxi during the Civil War, 1947*

These instructions were designed to fulfil Mao's promise that the 'army and the people are one'. Mao believed that the PLA had a vital political role to play in spreading communist ideology in areas that they occupied, and he also believed that actions were as important as words in convincing people that the Communists genuinely offered a better future.

Mao's communist guerrillas also appealed to the peasants on another level. Many peasants were nationalistic in their outlook, desiring a China that was free and independent of foreign interference and control. They especially supported the national struggle against the Japanese invaders. Mao's Communists were able to present themselves as a truly patriotic fighting force, in contrast with Chiang's nationalist forces which depended on American aid and had weakened the struggle against the Japanese by fighting against the Communists.

Land reforms

In areas controlled by the Communists, land reforms were introduced to benefit the poorest peasants and win their support for the communist cause. In Yan'an in the 1930s, for example, confiscation of land from the landlords and wealthier peasants and its redistribution among the poorest peasants had helped to cement popular support for the Communists in the countryside. During the Second World War, however, in order to maintain a United Front with the Nationalists against Japan, the Communists moderated their land reform programme. They implemented rent reductions and taxed richer peasants so that they were forced to sell off some of their land to poorer peasants, rather than antagonising the landlords by forcibly confiscating their land. In 1945, therefore, Mao was taking a cautious approach to land reform.

Rent reduction must be the result of mass struggle, not a favour from the government. Only then can we persuade the masses and enable them to understand that it is in the interests of the peasants and the people as a whole to allow the landlords to make a living so that they will not help the GMD. The present policy of our Party is still to reduce rents, not to confiscate land.

5	*Mao's land reform policy, November 1945. From **Selected Works of Mao Tse-tung***

As the Civil War got under way and the PLA began to occupy new areas, land reform policy became more radical.

After the Japanese surrender the peasants urgently demanded land and we made a timely decision to change our policy from reducing rent and interest to confiscating the land of the landlord class for distribution among the peasants. The Outline Land Law provides for equal distribution of land per head based on the principle of abolishing the land system of feudal exploitation and putting into effect the system of land to the tillers. To carry out the land reform resolutely and thoroughly it is necessary to organise in the villages first of all poor peasants' leagues composed of poor peasants and farm labourers and their elected committees.

6	*Mao's land reform policy, December 1947. From **Selected Works of Mao Tse-tung***

In 1946, when the Civil War began, the Communists returned to their more radical policy of confiscation of large estates in their 'land to the tillers' programme. In other words, the Party reverted to class struggle and began to move away from the United Front policies pursued earlier. Violence was an integral part of this process. At village rallies organised by CPC cadres, landlords and richer peasants were denounced and subjected to humiliation and violence. In many cases whole families were the victims – the children of landlords were labelled 'little landlords'. By early 1948, the campaign of terror had become so violent that some CPC members began to petition Mao for restraint. Mao called a halt, claiming that the excesses had been due to the mistakes of lower level communist officials.

The fear of revenge by landlords if the GMD recaptured control of an area also pushed the peasants towards supporting the Communists. The GMD used landlords' militias to regain control of villages. Once back under control, landlords exacted revenge on peasants who had participated in land reform. The land was forcibly taken back, rent arrears were collected at gunpoint and there were executions. In some cases landlords executed one member of every family that had participated in land reform.

Activity

Challenge your thinking

'Land reform was the key to the Communists' success in the Civil War.' Explain why you agree or disagree with this statement.

Cross-reference

Details on **Party cadres** can be found on page 43.

Exploring the detail

The reign of terror

It has been estimated that as many as 16 million people were subjected to some degree of physical abuse or humiliation, with the numbers killed running into hundreds of thousands. In one village in Shandong province in 1948, 120 people were beaten to death, including two boys aged seven.

Fig. 5 *A painting showing peasants denouncing a landlord during a land reform campaign*

■ **Exploring the detail**

Labourers in Manchuria

In Manchuria the CPC conscripted 1.6 million labourers who were employed in digging trenches, demolishing captured fortifications and transporting ammunition and the wounded. These peasant auxiliaries were crucial to the PLA in freeing regular troops to concentrate on fighting.

Under pressure from both Communists and Nationalists, and with the incentive of land reform, it was not surprising that the ranks of the PLA were swelled with new recruits from the peasants. The PLA also relied on a vast army of peasant auxiliaries to support the regular troops.

■ The reasons for the ultimate Communist victory

Fig. 6 *People in Nanjing await the arrival of PLA troops, April 1949*

The Communist victory in 1949 was primarily a military victory. Any explanation of the reasons for this victory, therefore, must begin with an examination of the tactics and strategy of the PLA. In such a complex historical event as the Chinese Civil War, however, a range of other factors – political, economic, social and diplomatic – played their part in determining the final outcome. We have already seen in Chapter 1 how, despite the larger size of the nationalist forces in 1946, the Communists started the war with several advantages over their opponents. As the war went on, nationalist weaknesses and communist strengths had a decisive impact on the outcome of the war.

Military factors

In the war against the Japanese the Communists had learned valuable lessons in how to fight against numerically superior forces. Guerrilla warfare had proved to be highly effective against the Japanese and was to be equally successful against the Nationalists in Manchuria, an area that was geographically well suited for this type of warfare because of its hilly terrain and large forested areas. Mao had written in the 1930s that,

Fig. 7 *Mao believed that guerrilla warfare was like the battle between an elephant and a tiger. In a straight battle, the elephant would win because of its size. If the tiger, however, kept attacking and then running, the elephant would eventually die from blood loss and exhaustion*

The basis of guerrilla war is to spread out and arouse the masses [to join in the struggle], and concentrate regular forces only when you can destroy the enemy. Fight when you know you can win. Don't fight battles you may lose.

In their operations guerrilla units have to concentrate the maximum forces, act secretly and swiftly, attack the enemy by surprise and bring battles to a quick decision. The basic principle of guerrilla warfare must be offensive and guerrilla warfare is more offensive in its character than regular warfare. The offensive, moreover, must take the form of surprise attacks.

7   *By Chairman Mao.*
From Selected Works
of Mao Tse-tung

when fighting a superior enemy, communist forces should establish base areas in the mountains and fight a campaign of surprise attacks against the enemy's weakest points. Using these tactics of 'wear and tear', the Communists were able to pick off nationalist units one by one, thereby gradually reducing their numerical advantage. They were also able to seize the initiative in the war, dominating rural areas and striking at vital communications routes such as railway lines, while the GMD forces were increasingly isolated in their city strongholds.

Communist military leadership

In Lin Biao, Mao had a military commander of outstanding ability. During 1947 he successfully transformed the PLA into a conventional army. The PLA absorbed much of the army of the Manchukuo puppet government in Manchuria and increased its strength with new recruits from peasant supporters. Later in the war, the PLA's main source of new troops was from nationalist units that had surrendered. Through intensive training in the use of weapons captured from the enemy and political indoctrination of the troops at large rallies, the PLA became a formidable fighting force. Lin Biao and the other PLA commanders moved over to an offensive strategy which brought victory first in Manchuria and later in northern, central and finally southern China.

Table 2 *Estimated strength of nationalist and communist forces in China, June 1948*

	Nationalists	Communists (PLA)
Troops	2,200,000	1,560,000
Artillery pieces	21,000	22,800

Note: These figures are estimates. Other sources have calculated that communist troop numbers in 1948 were much higher.

*Source: J. D. Spence, **The Search for Modern China**, 1990*

Nationalist errors

Chiang's first serious error was to send his best troops into Manchuria without securing complete control over northern and central China. In

■ **Activity**

Source analysis

Study Source 7 and figure 7.

1 What were the basic principles of guerrilla warfare as outlined by Mao?

2 Why was it necessary for the PLA to adopt guerrilla warfare at the start of the Civil War?

■ **Exploring the detail**

The Manchukuo puppet government

After the Japanese invasion of Manchuria in 1931, the Japanese renamed the area Manchukuo and established a government that was under their control.

■ **Activity**

Revision exercise

Using information in this chapter, summarise the main reasons why the Communists had been able to increase their military strength.

Manchuria his forces were spread too thinly, their supply lines were too long and they were highly vulnerable to the Communists' guerrilla warfare. The loss of Manchuria in early 1948 was a crucial defeat for Chiang. Corrupt and incompetent leadership of GMD forces also played its part in their defeat. A mainly conscript army, which was often left for days without adequate food and water, lacked fighting spirit; deaths from cold and hunger as well as desertions sapped the strength of nationalist forces and left many of them only too willing to surrender to the Communists.

Communist agents in the nationalist forces

Although nationalist troops often lacked the will to fight, many of their commanders were, in fact, communist agents. The nationalist commander in Manchuria, Wei Lihuang, was a communist agent who handed the initiative in this vital campaign to PLA forces and kept his forces in Manchuria long after their position had become hopeless, thereby ensuring that they suffered an even more catastrophic defeat. During the Beijing-Tianjin campaign, the nationalist commander Fu Zuoyi was loyal to Chiang Kai-shek but his daughter, who had access to all her father's campaign plans, was a communist agent who fed information to the PLA. In the battle for Nanjing, two senior nationalist generals, Lin Fei and Guo Rugui, were working for the Communists. The value to the Communists of having these 'moles' working at the highest levels in the GMD command was immense. The Nationalists, however, were unsuccessful in their efforts to infiltrate the Communists. Mao was innately suspicious and determined to root out any enemy agents. His ruthless use of terror to enforce control meant that there was no space within which agents could operate effectively.

Broadening the base of communist support

Under Mao's leadership, the Communists had concentrated on establishing themselves as a mainly peasant-based party. Communist policies of land reform were crucial in attracting peasant support for the Party. As peasants formed the vast majority of China's population, this was the best course of action for a party that aspired to be a mass movement. The PLA was largely made up of recruits from the peasants. The Communists' main bases were in the countryside. In order to take control over the government of China, however, it was necessary to take over the cities that were the centres of administration, industry, trade and communications.

During the course of the struggles against the Japanese and the Nationalists, the Party began to broaden the base of its supporters. In Manchuria during the Second World War, CPC members arrested by the Japanese came from a wide variety of occupations. They included peasant farmers, factory and railway workers, teachers, students and policemen. There were also some communist supporters among the middle classes who had been drawn to the Party by its patriotic record in the fight against the Japanese. Until the final stages of the Civil War, however, the CPC had only limited support in large cities. Although the Communists had infiltrated trades unions in large

■ Activity

Talking point

Discuss why the presence of communist agents at the highest levels in the nationalist forces gave the Communists such an advantage during the Civil War.

■ Cross-reference

For more on communist policies regarding **land reform**, see pages 26–8.

Fig. 8 *Tea leaf pickers in China – one aspect of Chinese agriculture*

industrial cities such as Shanghai and were able to use this to undermine the GMD by organising strikes, there was only limited CPC organisation in these cities before they were captured by the PLA.

From 1927 to the present the centre of gravity of our work has been in the villages. The period for this method of work has now ended. The period of the city leading the village has now begun. The centre of gravity of the Party's work has shifted from the village to the city.

8   *By Chairman Mao, 5 March 1949. From **Selected Works of Mao Tse-tung***

Having captured a city, however, the Communists were adept at attracting support through a variety of means. They were skilled at using newspapers, films and radio to spread communist propaganda. PLA troops were well disciplined and under orders not to loot and plunder the cities they captured – in marked contrast to the unruly behaviour of GMD troops. In the early stages of the war, Harbin in northern Manchuria was the only city controlled by the Communists; it was there that they learned how to administer a large urban area efficiently. Communist officials were effective in preventing crime, controlling the distribution of scarce food supplies and introducing a fair system of taxation. The experience gained in Harbin was then applied in other cities as they fell under communist control. By the spring of 1949, the PLA had captured so many cities that the Party had to reorientate its policies to reflect the changing situation. Now the priorities were to feed large urban populations, maintain production and prevent inflation of prices. Although they did not completely succeed in their efforts, their labours were praised by both foreign and Chinese observers.

Economic mismanagement by the nationalist government

15 May 1947. Rice prices have more than doubled in the past two weeks and the riots are spreading even to the countryside. Students and teachers are becoming increasingly violent and many heads were cracked in the Nanjing demonstrations today.

28 September 1947. (Shanghai) Big strikes started here yesterday and the city is half paralysed. Despite the current economic problems and the price jumps, the strikes are not economically motivated. Rather they are protests against the Guomindang and the secret police.

9   *A diary of life during the Civil War. From J. F. Melby, **The Mandate of Heaven**, 1968*

Serious mismanagement of the economy by the nationalist government weakened its support. In order to finance heavy expenditure on the Civil War, Chiang's government printed more bank notes. This had the effect of causing prices to rise and devaluing the currency:

■ By May 1946, prices had risen by 1,000 per cent over their September 1945 levels and the inflationary spiral continued to accelerate. In February 1947, the rate of inflation reached 3,000 per cent and during 1948 and 1949 the rate of price increases could be measured in the tens of thousands.

■ Those living on their savings and on fixed incomes were the worst hit by the inflation. Workers in large cities such as Shanghai could use their trades union organisations to strike for higher wages. The government's response was to attempt to buy off the workers through increased wages but this only forced manufacturers to put up prices even further.

Exploring the detail

The effects of inflation

The prices of basic foodstuffs show the effects of this inflation on ordinary consumers. In June 1948, a standard sack of flour sold for 6.7 million yuan; by August the price had risen to 63 million yuan.

■ Not until the summer of 1948 did Chiang's government take any decisive action to control the situation. In August 1948, the old bank notes in circulation were withdrawn and a new currency – the gold yuan – was introduced. The government also began to introduce rationing of food and other basic commodities, together with controls on wages and prices and new taxes. These reforms were too little, too late. Despite bringing a brief respite from inflation, the reforms failed and, by 1949, there was economic collapse in the areas controlled by the Nationalists. Paper money had become worthless and been replaced by a barter economy. Support for nationalist rule in China's large cities, even among the middle classes, was draining away long before the PLA captured control.

The role of foreign powers

American support for the Nationalists

Despite American reservations about Chiang Kai-shek, the USA provided financial and military assistance to the Nationalists. In total, the Americans gave nearly $3 billion in aid to the GMD government, in addition to the large quantities of arms they had supplied during the Second World War. The Americans transported nationalist troops by air and sea from their southern China bases to the north at the end of the war and American marines occupied Tianjin and Beijing temporarily until the arrival of nationalist forces. All of this was designed to forestall a communist takeover in the north at the end of the war. Despite this American assistance, however, the serious weaknesses in the nationalist regime and its armed forces led inexorably to the defeat of the Guomindang. Indeed, Mao was able to point to the fact that Chiang Kai-shek relied on American aid as evidence that China could never be truly independent under a nationalist government.

Soviet assistance to the Communists

Fig. 9 *On one of his rare visits outside China, Mao Zedong is seen at the 70th birthday celebration of Joseph Stalin in Moscow, December 1949*

In August 1945, Soviet troops occupied Manchuria. In some ways this was advantageous to the Chinese communists as they could expect to receive assistance from the Soviet Union. During the time they were occupying Manchuria – they remained until May 1946 – the Red Army provided much-needed training and equipment to the PLA. Many PLA officers were sent to Russia for training while, in Manchuria, the Red Army established 16 military training institutions including artillery and engineering schools. Captured Japanese arms and equipment were handed over to the PLA and released Japanese prisoners of war were employed in training Chinese pilots to fly. Soviet help was therefore vital to the PLA in helping it to transform itself into a formidable fighting machine. However, long-standing animosities between Mao and Stalin, the Soviet leader, were an obstacle to cooperation between them.

Soviet assistance, however, was not provided unconditionally. Stalin put the interests of the Soviet Union above those of the Chinese Communists. Anxious to avoid a confrontation with the USA, he did not wish to be seen to be giving assistance to the Chinese Communists. He also signed a treaty with Chiang Kai-shek in which he promised to hand over territory occupied by the Red Army to the Nationalists. In line with this policy, in November 1945 Soviet commanders in Manchuria ordered the PLA to withdraw from all major cities there. 'If you do not leave,' the Soviet commander told the Communists, 'we will use tanks to drive you out.' Isolated and under pressure from nationalist forces at the time, Mao had no choice but to comply. Later in the war, in the spring of 1949, Stalin urged Mao to consolidate his position in northern China and not send his forces across the Yangzi River into the south. Once again, Stalin was anxious to avoid American intervention in China's Civil War but, by this time, Mao was strong enough to defy Stalin. Having conquered Manchuria and northern and central China largely without Russia's assistance, he was no longer willing to be dictated to by Stalin.

Indirect American help to the Communists

Perhaps foreign intervention provided one vital lifeline to Mao. In the spring of 1946, communist forces in Manchuria were under severe pressure from the Nationalists. Having been forced by the Russians to abandon the cities, they had nevertheless hung on to Harbin but a renewed GMD offensive meant that they were on the point of abandoning this last city stronghold. At this point President Truman's envoy in China, George Marshall, persuaded Chiang to agree to a ceasefire. Initially meant to last two weeks, the ceasefire was extended to four months. During this vital breathing space the PLA was able to regroup, train its troops and organise its defences. When the Civil War resumed in October 1946, Chiang was unable to break the PLA defences in northern Manchuria.

Mao's leadership

Cross-reference

To recap on **George Marshall**, see page 14.

Questions

1 Did the Russians help or hinder the Chinese Communist Party in the Civil War?

2 What was the impact of foreign intervention on the outcome of the Chinese Civil War?

Fig. 10 *Mao Zedong embarks on a trip to meet Chiang Kai-shek for peace talks in 1945*

> Our principle is that the Party commands the gun and the gun must never be allowed to command the Party.

 By Chairman Mao. From Selected Works of Mao Tse-tung

From his base in Yan'an, and later Shensi, Mao orchestrated the campaigns of the PLA. By 1945 he was the undisputed leader of the CPC and, even from his remote headquarters, he was able to direct military operations. It was Mao who decided on the strategy of guerrilla warfare in the early stages of the war, he who announced the change to more conventional warfare in 1948 and it was again Mao who drew up the overall plans for the campaigns in the final stages of the war, although he left the details of the fighting to his commanders in the field. However, sometimes his over-riding self-confidence led him to make serious errors of judgement:

- In November 1945, he overruled his commander Liu Shaoqi and ordered PLA forces to defend the strategic pass between China and Manchuria against nationalist forces, a task for which they were neither equipped nor trained. Having been overrun by nationalist forces, the PLA was forced to fall back on Liu's original plan which was to concentrate its forces in northern Manchuria.

- Mao lacked experience in dealing with foreign powers, never having travelled beyond China's frontiers at this time. In 1945–6, he naively clung to the belief that the USA would force Chiang to form a coalition government with the CPC, thus avoiding a civil war, yet at the same time he was making plans to fight a civil war. During this year his policy was a series of bewildering zigzags from war to peace and back to war again.

Key profile

Liu Shaoqi

Originally from Henan province, Liu Shaoqi (1898–1969) had been trained in the USSR in the 1920s as a communist organiser and theorist. A close ally of Mao during the Yan'an years, Liu was an effective organiser of the communist resistance in north and central China. From 1943, Liu Shaoqi was recognised as Mao's chosen successor.

Fig. 11 *A Chinese postage stamp from 1965, commemorating the 30th anniversary of the Long March*

Nevertheless, through all of these twists and turns of his policies his position as Chairman of the CPC remained unchallenged. The personality cult surrounding Mao, which had been developing during the years he spent in Yan'an, gave him complete sway over the Communist Party and its military wing, the PLA.

Activity

Revision exercise

Copy and complete the table below, setting out the main factors that led to communist victory in the Civil War. Note that you will need to re-read parts of Chapter 1 as well as this chapter to help you complete this activity.

Factors	Nationalists	Communists
Military factors		
Political factors		
Economic factors		
Popular support		
International support		
Leadership		

Learning outcomes

In this section you have examined the relative strengths of the Communists and Nationalists in China at the end of the Second World War. You have also looked at the story of how the PLA won the Civil War and the range of factors that enabled the Communists to win. After reading this section, you should be able to identify the main causes of the communist victory and make an assessment of the relative importance of the different factors.

 Examination-style questions

(a) Explain why the Communists' guerrilla warfare strategy was effective in the war against the Guomindang.   *(12 marks)*

 Remember that these are essay-style questions and examiners will be looking for a clear line of argument running through your answers. The introduction should demonstrate that you have understood the question and that you are setting out the main argument that you are going to develop. Answers should be focused on the question throughout. This question requires you to show your knowledge and understanding of the guerrilla warfare strategy adopted by the Communists and explain why it was effective. This can be done in terms of an assessment of communist strengths and weaknesses and a comparison between these and the situation of the Guomindang armies. It would be useful to refer back to the Communists' use of guerrilla tactics against the Japanese and how this influenced the development of their military thinking.

(b) 'Mao's leadership was the crucial factor in leading the Communists to victory in the Civil War of 1946 to 1949.' Explain why you agree or disagree with this view.   *(24 marks)*

This question requires you to assess the importance of one factor – Mao's leadership – against a range of other factors. The examiner will be looking for both range of factors and balance in your answer. Your conclusion should summarise the argument you have been developing and offer some judgement in terms of whether Mao's leadership was more important than other factors in explaining the reasons for communist victory.

2 The consolidation of power, 1949–53

3 Mao and the Party

Fig. 1 *Mao Zedong announces the creation of the People's Republic of China, 1 October 1949. The group behind him includes Zhou Enlai, Lin Biao and Liu Shaoqi*

In this chapter you will learn about:

■ the ideology and leadership of Mao Zedong

■ the role of the Communist Party in the new government

■ the importance of mass Party membership in consolidating support for the regime

■ the part played by mass campaigns against corruption and the bourgeoisie in consolidating the regime.

At a ceremony on 1 October 1949, from a reviewing stand on top of the Gate of Heavenly Peace (Tiananmen), Beijing (once the entrance to the imperial palace), Mao Zedong announced the founding of the People's Republic of China. Shortly afterwards, both the new government and the Communist Party would take over the buildings to the left and right of the Forbidden City, while the residential area to the south would be demolished to make way for Tiananmen Square.

■ The ideology and leadership of Mao Zedong

Mao and Marxism

By 1949 Mao had established himself as the leader of the Chinese Communist Party. In the 28 years since he had joined the Party as a young activist he had developed his own, distinctive brand of revolutionary Communism. Over the years there had been many debates and divisions within the Party over ideological issues but, on many of the key issues, Mao's thinking had proved to be much more relevant to the situation in China than that of other leading Communists. This was largely because the leadership of the CPC in its early years had been in the hands of men who had been trained in revolutionary theory and practice in the Soviet Union. These '28 Bolsheviks', as they

were known, followed orthodox Marxist theory which emphasised
the importance of the industrial workers – the **proletariat** – in the
revolutionary class struggle that would lead eventually to a communist
society. Their priorities, therefore, were to build a Communist Party
membership in the cities among the workers in factories, transport
industries and mines. Mao, on the other hand, argued that industrial
workers were such a small minority in Chinese society – only 1 per
cent of the population in the early 1920s – that they could never form
the basis for a mass revolutionary party. Moreover, the Communist
Party was driven out of the cities by Chiang Kai-shek's forces after
1927. Mao believed that China's peasants, mostly poor and exploited
by the wealthy landlords, had the potential to become a revolutionary
force. All that was needed for this to happen, in Mao's view, was for
the Communist Party to work closely with the peasants and provide
them with revolutionary leadership. Mao's strategy of concentrating
on the rural areas proved to be the only realistic course of action open
to the CPC in the 1930s and 1940s; it ensured first the survival of the
Communist Party and later its eventual victory. It also helped to ensure
that Mao emerged from the various power struggles within the CPC as
the Chairman, and leading theorist, of the Party.

> **Key term**
>
> **Proletariat:** according to Marx, the working classes.

Fig. 2 *Marx and Mao*

Mao's position as Chairman of the Party was largely due to his role
as the leading theorist. Mao Zedong Thought had become the official
doctrine of the Communist Party. In government after 1949, Mao was
not involved in the day-to-day making and implementing of policy.
This he left to other leading Communists. He saw his role as being
to lead and keep alive an ideological debate within the Party over the
underlying principles on which policy should be based – what Mao
referred to as the 'general line'. By dominating the ideological debate
and periodically purging those people who were seen to be deviating

from the correct ideological path, Mao sought to control the Party and the government.

Mao Zedong Thought was a set of ideas that changed and adapted over time. Much of his ideology was based on Marxism but he adapted Marxism to Chinese conditions and added some ideas that were very much his own. The most important of these ideas were self-reliance, continuing revolution, class struggle, learning from the people and mass mobilisation.

Self-reliance

Mao was a Chinese nationalist as well as a revolutionary Communist. He shared with the Guomindang the desire for China to be restored as a powerful, independent nation because he had been deeply affected by China's humiliation at the hands of the Western powers and Japan during his youth. The revolution was fought to liberate China from foreign control as much as to free the people from **feudal landlords**. Once in power, Mao was determined that China should not be reliant on foreign powers. Although the communist government sought aid and advice from the Soviet Union in the 1950s, Mao was never comfortable with this unequal relationship and there were continuing divisions in the Communist Party over the extent to which China should follow the example of the Soviet Union in developing its economy.

Continuing revolution

For Mao, the revolution did not end when the Communist Party took power in 1949. Indeed, in many ways, the revolution was only just beginning. This was partly because, in the early years of communist rule, the class enemies – the landlords and the bourgeoisie – still owned most of the property in China and still largely controlled the economy. Mao also believed that commitment to the revolution's aims and values came largely through actual involvement in the revolutionary process itself; those who participated in violence against landlords and the confiscation of their property were more likely to fight to prevent a return to the old ways. Mao believed that it was essential for each new generation to be involved in revolutionary struggle, both to prevent the threat of a counter-revolution and to ensure their continuing support for the regime. Whereas many of Mao's colleagues believed that China needed political stability in order to achieve economic development, he always placed a higher priority on maintaining the revolutionary zeal of the masses.

Class struggle

For Mao, the revolution was essentially a class struggle and continuing this struggle was the key to maintaining the revolution. He believed that there was a danger that the Communist Party itself, once established in power, could become a new ruling class that could exploit the people in ways similar to the old ruling class. In power, communist officials would enjoy the benefits of rank and privilege that would detach them from the people they were supposed to serve. He therefore believed that the Communist Party needed to be periodically rectified, as had happened for the first time in the Yan'an Rectification campaign of 1942. During these campaigns, Party officials were subjected to **struggle meetings** at which they faced public criticism and were forced to make self-criticisms, after which many were made to undergo re-education by attending indoctrination meetings and working in the fields with the peasants.

Key terms

Feudal landlords: landlords in China had enormous power over their tenants (peasant farmers) through the collection of rents. Although this relationship was not 'feudal' in the European sense of the word (i.e. where peasants are bound in law to their lord), it became common practice for Communists in China to describe the landlord–tenant relationship as feudal in the sense that it was exploitative, unequal and outdated.

Struggle meetings: these were a method of putting anyone suspected of being in opposition to the regime under severe psychological pressure. Victims were forced to listen while their colleagues recounted their 'crimes' and were expected themselves to make full confessions and self-criticisms.

Cross-reference

For more information on the **bourgeoisie**, look back at page 22.

Exploring the detail

The Yan'an Rectification campaign

In this campaign Mao consolidated his leadership of the Party by forcing members, even at the most senior levels, to confess their past errors (of thought) and make a public statement of the correctness of Mao Zedong Thought. Many members suspected of 'errors' were publicly humiliated; some were tortured to confess their crimes, as a result of which a number died or committed suicide.

团结起来 争取更大的胜利

Fig. 3 *A Chinese propaganda poster showing Chairman Mao's leadership. The slogan reads 'Unite all to obtain greater victories'*

Learning from the people

Mao believed that the Communist Party should be embedded in the people; the Party should listen to the concerns of the people and learn from them. He also argued that the masses should participate in discussions on policy. In Mao's eyes, the people should act as a check on the power of the Communist Party, ensuring that its rule did not become dictatorial and unjust. Mao was determined that the Chinese Communist Party should not follow the example of the Soviet Union where the Communist Party behaved in a commandist way, issuing orders but not listening to the people's concerns.

Mass mobilisation

Mao argued that the Communist Party's main task in government was to mobilise the people in mass campaigns to achieve specific objectives. He had a firm faith in the essential goodness of the people and believed that China's millions, once mobilised and enthused with revolutionary zeal, could achieve anything. Mass mobilisation might be used, therefore, to carry out major works such as the building of dams or roads, the cultivation of areas not previously used for farming or even major industrial projects. Mao did not believe that managers and experts were the key to economic advance. Nor did he accept that people needed to be offered extra money to persuade them to work harder. Once the Party had convinced the people of the superiority of Socialism, he believed that people would willingly work harder for the greater common good.

Mao was the Chairman of the Communist Party and its chief ideologist. In a party as large as the Communist Party, however, it was perhaps inevitable that not every leading figure was in total agreement with Mao.

Exploring the detail

The Soviet model for economic development

As the USSR was the first country to adopt a communist system, Communists in other countries looked to the USSR as a model for their own development. From 1928, under Stalin's ruthless leadership, the USSR had embarked on a series of Five Year Plans that transformed it from a mainly agricultural society to a major industrial power. The plans placed a high priority on the development of 'heavy' industries such as iron and steel production, engineering and energy production. At the same time, peasant farmers were forced to abandon their small private plots and join large collective farms.

Activity

Revision exercise

Summarise the main ideas in Mao Zedong Thought under the following headings: Self-reliance; Continuing revolution; Class struggle; The role of the peasants; The role of the Party; Mass mobilisation.

There had been splits and divisions before the Communist Party came to power in 1949, and there would be many disagreements and debates once it was the Party of government. Mao sometimes experienced difficulty in getting his ideas accepted. In these circumstances he needed to fall back on another key aspect of his personality – his flexibility. For Mao, the key to his earlier successes had been his ability to work out what course of action would be best suited to a particular set of circumstances. Sometimes this led him to make tactical alliances with groups that could be useful to him. In the struggle against the Japanese he was prepared to cooperate with the Guomindang and even the landlords in order to build a United Front. Once the Japanese had been defeated, the priority changed and Mao concentrated on defeating the Guomindang in order to win power. He used the same tactical flexibility in his dealings with his own party. If one group of leading Communists were reluctant to follow his ideas, he turned to others, or even groups outside the Party, to get his way. For Mao, his ideological goals were fixed; tactics, however, were fluid.

The role of the Communist Party in the new government

The challenges facing the new government in 1949

In 1949, China's economy and its people were exhausted after years of war and conflict. China had been through decades of internal conflict culminating in the Civil War of 1946–9. In addition to this there had been eight years of war against the Japanese occupation. These years of conflict had left a damaging legacy for the new government:

- As peasants had been taken away from their farms to fight in these wars, agricultural production had fallen and food shortages were a serious problem in urban areas. Industrial production had also fallen.
- The nationalist Guomindang government had left a legacy of soaring inflation and the financial situation had been made worse by Guomindang officials taking all of China's reserves of foreign currency with them when they fled to Taiwan.
- Internationally, the communist victory had created a rift between China and the Western powers; cut off from trade and contact with the West, China's only source of foreign assistance was the Soviet Union.
- Internally, the new government was not yet in full control of all areas of China, particularly the outlying provinces and semi-autonomous regions. No government since 1911 had succeeded in breaking down the power of local warlords or overcoming China's deep social and ethnic divisions. If the new government were to succeed in its aim of transforming Chinese society, it would need to build a new sense of national unity in which the diverse elements of Chinese society were brought into line with the new political direction of the State.

In the short-term, the priority for the new government was to stabilise the economic and political situation and extend its control. It did this in a number of ways:

- Inflation was brought under control through strict regulation of the economy; public expenditure was cut, taxes were raised and a new currency – the renminbi – was introduced.
- The property of Guomindang supporters who had fled to Taiwan was confiscated by the State.
- All foreign assets in China, apart from those of the Soviet Union, were confiscated.

Did you know?

Ethnic groups

Most Chinese refer to themselves as 'Han' Chinese to distinguish them from other ethnic groups in China. Other minority ethnic groups in China include Manchus, Mongols, Uighurs and Tibetans.

■ The banks, gas and electricity supply and transport industries were nationalised.

■ In three 'reunification' campaigns in 1950 and 1951, the PLA established central government control in three regions: Xizang (Tibet), Xinjiang and Guangdong.

■ A new system of government was established in which the dominant position of the Communist Party was legitimised.

Although many of these measures were radical in themselves, the general tone of the new government's approach in its early years was one of caution. Mao made clear that the ultimate aim of the regime was to build a communist society in China but, according to Marxist-Leninist theory, China was not yet at the stage of development when Communism was possible. In order to develop agriculture and industry, Mao recognised that the communist regime would need the support of the 'national bourgeoisie' – the factory owners, businessmen and the intelligentsia. It was the educated middle classes who provided the personnel for government officials and factory managers. Therefore, Mao tried to build the new regime on a broad foundation and pursued policies that would not alienate potential middle-class supporters. For example, shareholders and owners of enterprises that were nationalised were given compensation as long as they were willing to cooperate with the regime. He was also prepared to tolerate the existence of other political parties: 14 parties (excluding the CPC) participated in the Chinese People's Political Consultative Conference in September 1949. However, these parties were only tolerated as long as they did not threaten the CPC's grip on power.

In pursuing these policies, Mao was continuing and building on the 'general line' which, under his leadership, the CPC had been following in Yan'an since 1936. Under this policy, which Mao sometimes referred to as a United Front policy, he invited the national bourgeoisie and landlords to participate in building a new China under the leadership of the CPC.

A 'people's democratic dictatorship'

> All the experience the Chinese people have accumulated through several decades teaches us to enforce the people's democratic dictatorship; that is, to deprive the reactionaries of the right to speak and let the people alone have that right. Who are the people? At the present stage in China, they are the working class, the peasantry, the urban petty bourgeoisie, and the national bourgeoisie. These classes, led by the working class and the Communist Party, unite to form their own State and elect their own government. Democracy is practised within the ranks of the people, who enjoy the right of free speech, assembly, association and so on. The right to vote belongs only to the people, not to the reactionaries. The combination of these two aspects, democracy for the people and dictatorship over the reactionaries, is the people's democratic dictatorship.

1   *Mao Zedong on the people's democratic dictatorship, 1949.*
From Selected Works of Mao Tse-tung

The new system of government for the People's Republic of China contained three separate but parallel strands:

■ The State bureaucracy at national, regional and local levels.

■ The Communist Party at national, regional and local levels.

■ The People's Liberation Army.

Activity

Preparing a presentation

'In view of the scale of the problems facing the new communist government after 1949, the cautious approach taken by Mao was the only realistic policy.' Divide the class into two groups. One group should prepare a presentation in support of this proposition and the other should prepare a presentation giving an alternative point of view.

Exploring the detail

Political parties in China

The more important of these non-communist parties included the Revolutionary Committee of the China Guomindang (which had broken away from the main GMD), the China Democratic League, the China Democratic National Construction Association, China Peasants' and Workers' Democratic Party and the China Zhi Gong Dang. These, and other parties, are still in existence and participate in China's political structures. However, they were subjected to persecution during the purges of the 1950s and 1960s.

Exploring the detail

The 'New Democracy'

Mao referred to the system of government established in 1949 as the 'New Democracy'. It was based on the system he had adopted in Yan'an between 1936 and 1945. This system was based on the belief that China was not yet ready for a fully fledged socialist system and that a transition stage was needed to bridge the gap between China's old, semi-feudal system and the eventual establishment of a socialist system. As the working class (proletariat) were not sufficiently large or strong to rule alone, they would have to do so in coalition with other classes, which in China comprised the peasants, the petty bourgeoisie and the national bourgeoisie. These four classes constituted the 'people' and only the people could participate in the political life of the PRC and be granted any political rights. Other classes were called the 'five black categories': 'reactionary elements', 'feudal elements', 'lackeys of imperialism', 'bureaucratic capitalists' and 'enemies of the people'. These groups were classified as non-people, lacking any political rights but nevertheless subject to the laws of the State. They were to be repressed, punished or reformed.

Cross-reference

See page 49 for more on **Zhou Enlai**.

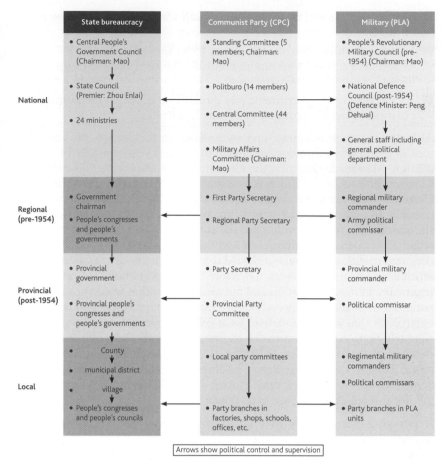

Arrows show political control and supervision

Fig. 4 *Communist political control over the People's Republic of China*

Figure 4 shows that the Communist Party was at the heart of the government structure in the new PRC. Leading members of the Party held all of the key posts in both the government and the PLA. All the important debates about policy and all the key decisions were taken by the Party's Standing Committee, itself a select group taken from the larger Politburo. At the apex of the whole structure stood Chairman Mao.

Below the level of central government, the Communist Party dominated the government of the provinces and local administration in towns and villages. Gao Gang, a Politburo member, was the provincial governor in Manchuria, a job he combined with being Party Chairman and military commander in the same area. Deng Xiaoping in the south-west, Peng Dehuai in the north-west and Lin Biao in the central southern region all combined political and military commands.

Key profile

Deng Xiaoping

The son of a peasant from Sichuan, Deng Xiaoping (1904–97) joined the CPC while he was in France in the 1920s on a work-study programme. He also studied in Moscow in 1926–7. He was a veteran of the Long March, a long-standing ally of Mao and served as a military leader in the PLA during the Civil War. By the 1950s he was recognised as a leading figure in the CPC hierarchy and became the Party's General Secretary in 1957.

In theory there were representative assemblies within this structure that brought a democratic element to the constitution. A Political Consultative Conference was held in 1949 to formally establish the new republic. Within the Party structure there was the national Party Congress that brought together representatives from Party branches from all over the country to debate policy issues and make decisions. However, this Congress met infrequently. After 1949, the next Congress was not called until 1956. Even when Congresses did meet, they merely agreed the policies that had already been decided by the Politburo.

Mass Party membership

Membership of the CPC stood at 4,448,000 in October 1949. By December 1950 this had increased to 5,821,604. In a country of about 500 million people, therefore, Party membership was very much the preserve of a small minority. Following the Leninist concept of an elite vanguard party, membership of the CPC was restricted to those who could demonstrate their commitment and ideological correctness. Within the larger membership there was an even more select group of Party **cadres**.

Fig. 5 *Mao Zedong with members of the Chinese People's Political Consultative Committee, June 1950*

Party cadres permeated all levels of government and administration, the legal system, schools and colleges and the PLA. Through them the CPC was able to ensure that both the governmental system and the armed forces were operating strictly in accordance with the political direction of the State. The CPC established branches in all aspects of national life such as factories, shops, schools, offices, neighbourhoods and PLA units. CPC members also took leading roles in various mass organisations including trades unions, the All-China Federation of Democratic Youth and the All-China Federation of Women. At a local level there were many 'mass autonomous organisations' through which the CPC sought to involve 'the masses' in its efforts to transform society. Urban neighbourhood committees, public security committees and people's mediation committees took on responsibility for matters of public health, policing and the resolution of disputes, all under the watchful eyes of the CPC and its cadres. These mass organisations channelled the energies of the Chinese people and encouraged a sense of participation in building a new and better society, but their activities were closely scrutinised and directed by the Communist Party.

At the base of the governmental pyramid in the new China was the *danwei* or work unit. Every employed Chinese citizen living in an urban area belonged to a work unit; those who did not work came under the supervision of a residents' committee. The work units, led by Party cadres, controlled the allocation of housing, grain, cooking oil and cloth. The work unit also issued permits to travel, marry, enter the army or university and change employment.

Party cadres enjoyed a privileged lifestyle compared to that of ordinary Chinese citizens. For those who had 'joined the revolution', the CPC functioned as a kind of family unit. In return for absolute loyalty to the head of the family, the Party provided for its members. Under a system known as the 'iron rice-bowl', party and government officials, employees of State-run enterprises and military personnel were guaranteed employment and an income for life.

The role of the People's Liberation Army

By 1950, the People's Liberation Army had become an enormous military force. With 5 million men under its command and its efforts to build a new air force and navy, spending on the PLA accounted for over 41 per cent of the total State budget. It was clear to China's communist rulers that, if China were to be able to afford to spend money on economic development, expenditure on the armed forces would need to be reduced. It was also necessary to release men from military service so that they could engage in productive work. Therefore, in 1950 it was decided to begin a partial demobilisation of the PLA, which resulted in a reduction in size to some 3.5 million men by 1953. Even after these cuts, however, the PLA still received 800,000 new conscripts every year, each man serving for three years. This meant that the PLA was still the largest army in the world. It also meant that millions of young Chinese men passed through the PLA's ranks, emerging after three years having been trained in warfare and indoctrinated in the ideology of the Communist Party.

The PLA occupied a special place in the mythology of the Chinese communist revolution. In the struggles against the Japanese and later against the Guomindang, the PLA's soldier-heroes had come to epitomise the revolutionary virtues cultivated by Mao: discipline, self-sacrifice, endurance and perseverance against overwhelming odds. These were

Activity

Thinking point

1 By what means did the CPC control the following at all levels?

a The system of government.

b Chinese society.

A spider diagram showing the connections between the CPC and the system of government could help to clarify this.

2 How did the CPC ensure continuing loyalty and commitment from its members?

Activity

Source analysis

Go to **www.iisg.nl/~landsberger** and find the section showing PLA propaganda posters.

1 What image(s) of PLA soldiers are being presented in these posters?

2 Using the posters and the information in this book, show how the PLA was used as a role model for civilians in the new communist China.

the virtues that Mao wished to instil in the Chinese population at large and PLA troops were held up as role models for others to emulate. These virtues were again demonstrated by Chinese troops during the Korean War (1950–3) when 'volunteer' units of the PLA fought against American, British and other international forces. The endurance and heroism of Chinese troops in Korea was celebrated by a number of films, plays and works of literature.

As well as having a propaganda value, the PLA could be put to more practical uses in China itself. As all military units had political commissars embedded with them, PLA troops were thoroughly well indoctrinated in communist ideology. Part of their role in the countryside was to pass on that communist ideology to the peasants. They were also put to work on many public works projects such as rebuilding bridges, roads and railways that had been damaged in the wars. Some demobilised PLA units were actually restructured for this new role. The First Field Army, based in Xinjiang, became the Production and Construction Army with the task of developing untapped mineral resources and agricultural land.

Fig. 6 *Mao Zedong delivers a speech at a workers', peasants' and soldiers' conference, September 1950*

Mass campaigns against corruption and the bourgeoisie

Repression and terror were key weapons in the CPC's struggle to control the population of China after the formation of the People's Republic in 1949. At first Mao pursued a cautious policy in order to build and maintain a broad coalition of support. By the end of 1950, however, the outbreak of the Korean War engendered both a heightened sense of national unity and a feeling that China's revolution was under threat from both internal and external forces. This atmosphere, which was deliberately encouraged by Mao and the CPC, was used to justify more extreme measures against 'counter-revolutionary elements' and thus allowed Mao to move faster in his efforts to establish a dictatorship.

The machinery of repression used by the State included propaganda campaigns to isolate and shame the chosen targets, the police, the courts (although these were increasingly replaced by Communist Party committees), imprisonment and executions. A large network of forced labour camps (known as *lao-gai*, meaning 'reform through labour') was set up, much as had been done in the Soviet Union under Stalin. Under Mao's direction, repression and terror in China involved the whole population, using the same methods as those employed in the public health campaigns and land reform. A nationwide network of work units, street and neighbourhood committees was established to assist the CPC in its efforts not only to identify and punish all those suspected of counter-revolutionary crimes but also to exert control over the whole population.

By the summer of 1951, all Chinese citizens over the age of 15 had to acquire official residence permits from the police and obtain permission if they wished to move to another area. Every citizen came under the scrutiny of their neighbours and workmates and people were encouraged to inform on each other. Prostitution was virtually stamped out by 1953 through the work of street committees in placing brothels

Exploring the detail

Labour camps

With advice from Russian experts, the regime established the *lao-gai* as prisons. Perhaps millions of Chinese were sent to these camps, which were often in harsh environments, for hard physical labour in the fields or mines. Harry Wu and Carolyn Wakeman (*Bitter Winds*, 1994) have estimated that were over 1,000 camps by the late 1960s, whereas Chang and Halliday (*Mao: The Unknown Story*, 2006) have estimated that as many as 27 million people were either executed, committed suicide or worked to death in the camps.

■ **Activity**

Thinking point

What had been gained and what had been lost by Chinese citizens as a result of Mao's attempts to tighten communist control over Chinese society?

under surveillance; many prostitutes and their pimps were sent to 're-education' centres as punishment. Similarly, drug dealing and addiction was clamped down on; dealers were shot, addicts had their supply of drugs withdrawn and their families were made responsible for their future behaviour. Tobacco production was placed under a government monopoly and the population was encouraged to smoke cigarettes. Through ruthlessness and careful organisation, much of the crime that had plagued China's cities in the years before 1949 was stamped out and, in the process, the Communist Party increased its control over Chinese society.

There were four mass campaigns in the years 1950–2 through which Mao and the CPC pressed down on Chinese society.

The Resist America and Aid Korea campaign

After China and the USA become involved in the armed conflict in Korea in October 1950, foreigners in general and Americans in particular became identified as enemies of the PRC. Westerners who stayed in China became the targets of persecution. Many foreigners, including missionaries, were arrested and charged with being spies. Christian churches were forcibly closed, their property seized and priests and nuns expelled from the country. By the end of 1950, most foreigners, except those from the Soviet Union, had left China and the country once again became closed to Western influences. The campaign also targeted those Chinese suspected of spying for foreign powers. Any institution that had Western links, such as businesses, universities and churches, came under suspicion. Police searches led to the confiscation of radios and weapons kept at home, while mass rallies were organised to draw ordinary Chinese citizens into the growing frenzy of suspicion.

The Suppression of Counter-revolutionaries campaign

Launched in October 1950 and lasting for over a year, this campaign focused on the internal threats to the Chinese revolution. The definition of 'counter-revolutionary' included anyone who had had links with the GMD regime as well as 'bandits' (those in criminal gangs) and members of religious sects. With such a wide-ranging list of targets, large numbers of Chinese were denounced, investigated and punished. In Shanghai, for example, the authorities claimed to have uncovered evidence against 40,000 people; in Guangdong 52,620 'bandits' and 89,701 other criminals were caught, resulting in 28,332 people being executed in less than a year. Many of the executions were carried out in public to have maximum impact. Mao ordered his police chief to send reports on the progress of the campaign directly to him and he tried to exercise close control over the level of executions.

> If we are weak and indecisive and excessively indulgent of evil people, it will bring disaster.

2   *Chairman Mao, January 1951. From **Selected Works of Mao Tse-tung***

> Persons who have to be executed to assuage the people's anger must be put to death for this purpose.

3   *Chairman Mao, June 1952. From **Selected Works of Mao Tse-tung***

■ **Key term**

Assuage: Verb meaning 'to satisfy' or 'to make less intense'.

Mao intended most of the population – children and adults alike – to witness violence and killing. His aim was to scare and brutalise the entire population in a way that went much further than either Stalin or Hitler, who largely kept their foulest crimes out of sight.

4
Adapted from Jung Chang and J. Halliday,
Mao: The Unknown Story, 2006

Activity

Source analysis

Study Sources 2, 3 and 4. What can we learn from these sources about the political value of violence in China in the early 1950s?

Cross-reference

See page 38 for more on the **Yan'an Rectification campaign**.

The Three-Antis campaign

This campaign was started in Manchuria in late 1951 and was then extended to the rest of the country. Its targets were corruption, waste and obstructionist bureaucracy and those in the firing line were managers, State officials and Party members. As with earlier campaigns, it involved mass meetings at which officials and managers were denounced, investigations by Party committees and the eventual humiliation of those found guilty. Following the methods used in 1942 in the Yan'an Rectification campaign, Party members were forced to subject themselves to self-criticism and face group pressure to 'rectify' their errors of thought or deed. The campaign succeeded in rooting out many of the corrupt practices which had been the norm in Chinese business and public administration, such as bribery and influence. Party members were given a sharp reminder of the dangers of independent thought.

The Five-Antis campaign

Launched in January 1952, this campaign was directed against the bourgeoisie. It targets were bribery, tax evasion, the theft of State property, cheating on government contracts and economic espionage. Workers' organisations were enlisted by the Party to investigate their employers' business affairs. Group criticism sessions were organised for employers either to confess their own crimes or to denounce others. Mass meetings, of which there were 3,000 in February 1952 in Shanghai alone, were the scenes for public denunciations. Those found guilty faced enormous fines, the confiscation of their property and being sent to labour camps. Although executions were not a major feature of either the Three-Antis or the Five-Antis campaigns, many of those denounced committed suicide. It has been estimated that as many as 2 to 3 million took their own lives rather than face further humiliation.

The party's all-round intrusion into people's lives was the very point of the process known as 'thought reform'. Mao wanted not only external discipline, but the total subjection of all thoughts, large or small. Every week a meeting for 'thought examination' was held for those 'in the revolution'. Everyone had to criticise themselves for incorrect thoughts and be subjected to the criticism of others. The meetings tended to be dominated by self-righteous and petty-minded people, who used them to vent their envy and frustration. Meetings were an important means of communist control. They left people no free time and eliminated private thoughts.

5
*Adapted from Jung Chang, **Wild Swans**, 1992*

In the first four years after the communist victory in 1949, the Communist Party firmly entrenched itself as the governing party in the new People's Republic of China. At all levels and in all provinces

■ **Activity**

Talking point

'By 1953, China was well on the way to becoming a totalitarian regime.' Organise a class debate on this issue by dividing the class into two groups, one to speak in support of the proposition and the other to oppose it.

and regions (except Taiwan), the Communist Party established a firm grip on the government of China. Through the many mass campaigns the experience of participating in revolutionary activity was extended from the countryside to the cities and into all areas of Chinese life. In this way many more people than the relatively small CPC membership became committed to revolutionary struggle and the survival of the communist regime. Those who were not committed were repressed and terrorised to such effect that all signs of opposition had been eradicated.

■ Mao and the purges of the CPC: the purge of Gao Gang and Rao Shushi, 1953

In late 1953, Mao began the first major purge of leading CPC figures since the establishment of the People's Republic in 1949. The background to this purge was the launch of a Five Year Plan for the development of Chinese industry in 1953, which will be explored in more detail in Section 3. The decision to begin economic planning started a debate within the leading ranks of the Communist Party over the pace of the economic changes that the plan would bring about.

Gao Gang had become the leading CPC official in Manchuria in 1949, holding all four senior posts within the government, the Communist Party and the PLA in the region. With such a strong power base he was regarded as one of the CPC's rising stars and, in 1952, he became head of the Central Planning Commission which had responsibility for directing the First Five Year Plan. In the debate over the pace of change, Gao took the side of Mao and criticised Zhou Enlai and Liu Shaoqi for their more cautious approach. Believing that he had Mao's backing, and with the support of Rao Shushi (the CPC leader in the Shanghai region), Gao attempted to usurp the position of Zhou Enlai and become Vice-Chairman of the CPC. Alerted to Gao's intrigues by Deng Xiaoping (a leading figure in the CPC), Mao used the December 1953 meeting of the Politburo to accuse Gao and Rao of attempting to build independent kingdoms in their regions and of 'underground activities'. Early in 1954, Gao committed suicide rather than face humiliation and disgrace; Rao was arrested and died in prison some 20 years later.

■ **Cross-reference**

For more on **Liu Shaoqi**, see pages 34 and 99–101.

For more on **Deng Xiaoping**, see pages 42 and 99–101.

■ Key profiles

Gao Gang

One of the few communist leaders with little formal education, Gao Gang (1902–54) was virtually illiterate but proved himself to be an effective organiser. After joining the CPC in 1926, he was the local Party leader in Shanxi province before the arrival of the Long March. During the Civil War, he was in charge of planning the economic recovery of Manchuria and with this experience he rose to become head of the Central Planning Commission in 1952.

Rao Shushi

Rao (1903–75) joined the CPC in 1925 and worked first as a youth organiser and then as a trades union organiser in Shanghai. During the Civil War, Rao was the political commissar of the Shandong Field Army. After 1949, he became governor of the East China (Shanghai) region and rose in 1953 to become minister in charge of the Party's organisation department.

Zhou Enlai

Zhou Enlai (1898–1976) was the son of a minor civil servant from Jiangsu province. He rose to become one of the leading figures in the government of the Chinese People's Republic. After a university education in Japan, Zhou returned to China and was involved in the May 4th Movement in 1919. He was sent to France in the early 1920s on a work-study programme for Chinese students and helped to found the European branch of the Chinese Communist Party in Paris. Returning to China, he became a political commissar at the Whampoa Military Academy in 1925. In the early 1930s, Zhou often sided with the official leadership of the Party against Mao but, after Mao's victory in the leadership struggle, Zhou 'made a religion of loyalty to Mao' for the rest of his life. An effective administrator, and with personal experience of living in Europe, Zhou became Prime Minister in the new government with a particular interest in relations with foreign powers. In Chinese politics he was regarded as a voice of reason and pragmatism within the Communist Party.

This episode demonstrated once again to the CPC's leading cadres that there were limits to the scope for debate within the Communist Party. Mao's position had been further strengthened whereas Zhou Enlai and Liu Shaoqi had been given a reminder that, in contrast to Mao, they were expendable.

Fig. 7 *Chairman Mao, with other leading communists, at a meeting to draft a new constitution for the PRC in March 1954*

Cross-reference

For details on the purge of
Peng Dehuai, see pages 86–7.

A closer look

Mao and the purges of the Communist Party

Mao had purged political opponents from the Party leadership on earlier occasions – for example, during the Yan'an years – and he would purge other opponents in the future. There would be another purge (of Peng Dehuai) in 1959. Mao would also engage in a long power struggle with Liu Shaoqi and Deng Xiaoping in the early 1960s, which would culminate in the Cultural Revolution of 1966. Purging opponents became a regular and necessary method by which Mao exercised his dominance over the Party.

Summary questions

1. How successful was the Communist Party in establishing its control over the lives of ordinary Chinese citizens in the years from 1949 to 1953?

2. How successful was Mao in dealing with challenges to his authority from within the Communist Party?

4 Reforming China

In this chapter you will learn about:

- the process of land reform and how this affected Chinese peasants

- how the Chinese revolution changed the role and status of women

- the progress made in establishing a system of universal education in China

- the progress made in improving public health.

Fig. 1 *A propaganda poster, 'New books for the State farm', reflecting educational and propagandist work by the Communists among the peasants*

> As the train approached Chengdu in the early afternoon, [my mother] found herself increasingly looking forward to a new life there. She was twenty-two. At the same age, some twenty years before, her mother had been living as a virtual prisoner in Manchuria in a house belonging to her absent warlord 'husband', under the watchful eyes of his servants; she was the plaything and the property of men. My mother, at least, was an independent human being. Whatever her misery, she was sure it bore no comparison with the plight of her mother as a woman in old China. She told herself she had a lot to thank the Chinese Revolution for.

1   *From Jung Chang, **Wild Swans**, 1992*

As a young revolutionary student in 1919, Mao had concluded that in order to change China it was necessary to change society. To change society it was necessary to change the system and to change the system it was essential to take power. In 1949, with power in his grasp, Mao Zedong began to attempt to change many aspects of Chinese society.

The Chinese People's Political Consultative Committee, which had met in September 1949, drew up a Common Programme for China setting out an agenda for political, economic and social change. Article 5 of the programme guaranteed to all, except 'political reactionaries', the rights of freedom of thought, speech, publication, assembly, association, correspondence, the person, domicile, movement, religious belief and the freedom to hold processions and demonstrations. The programme promised economic change through land reform and the development of heavy industry. Social change was highlighted in two key clauses: the promise of equal rights for women and an end to their lives of 'bondage', and the emphasis on the need for universal, free education.

In rural China, the possession of land gave life: if you had fields, you could eat; without fields, you would starve. Among a nation of four hundred million, 90 per cent of whom were peasants, land redistribution – taking from the rich and giving to the poor – was the primary vehicle carrying the revolution forward.

| 2 | *From P. Short,* **Mao: A Life**, *1999* |

■ Exploring the detail

Executions

Estimates vary as to how many actually died in this wave of land seizures in the early 1950s. Official Chinese estimates put the figure at around 700,000, whereas Chang and Halliday (*Mao: The Unknown Story*, 2006) estimate that the true figure was nearer 3 million. Mao wanted the executions to have maximum impact by involving peasants in the killing and having the executions carried out in public.

■ Key term

The means of production: Marx used this phrase to refer to factories, mines, transport systems and land; in other words, the economic resources that produce the wealth of the people.

■ Land reforms

Land confiscation

Before 1949, in areas controlled by the Communists, land reform was the essential means by which the Communist Party had gained the support of the peasants. Once the CPC had taken control of the whole of China, land reform was extended to the whole country. No longer did Mao veer between rent reductions and land confiscation, as he had done in 1946–9. Once the Communists were in power, land reform meant nothing more nor less than the confiscation and redistribution of land to poorer peasants and landless labourers. On the other hand, Mao was careful to ensure that it was only land belonging to the rich landlords that was confiscated; the holdings of better-off peasants were left untouched because Mao recognised that the food produced by the wealthier peasants was essential to the nation as a whole.

Starting in 'key point' villages, teams of 30 to 40 CPC cadres working with local peasants' associations fanned out across the countryside to carry the revolution to the more remote areas. Local peasants were encouraged to identify their landlords, who were then subjected to humiliation and violence. The CPC involved peasants in this process and deliberately stoked up class conflict between peasants and landlords in order to cement the relationship between China's peasants and the communist revolution. Many landlords and their relatives were sentenced to death.

> Peasants who killed with their bare hands the landlords who oppressed them were wedded to the new revolutionary order in a way that passive spectators could never be.

| 3 | *From P. Short,* **Mao: A Life**, *1999* |

The land confiscations of the early 1950s finally broke the power of the landlord class in the Chinese countryside. Indeed, with so many landlords being killed and their surviving relatives having been cowed into submission, the landlord class ceased to exist.

Moves towards cooperation

Redistribution of land left land ownership in private hands and peasant families free to cultivate their fields in the traditional way. In the long term it was the aim of the Communist Party to collectivise agriculture. Not only was this seen as the best way to bring more modern methods of farming to the Chinese countryside and thereby increase food production – an essential pre-requisite if China were to become more industrialised with a greater proportion of its population living in cities – it was also a basic tenet of Marxist theory that collective ownership of **the means of production** represented a more advanced stage of development than private, individual ownership. In the early 1950s, however, Mao believed that a policy of forcing peasants into larger collective farms or communes would encounter resistance and threaten to undermine peasant support for the revolution. Only the most

Fig. 2 *Mao Zedong (left) at a village in Shunyi, 1954. Photographs showing Mao participating in manual labour were used to strengthen his image as a man of the people*

cautious moves towards cooperation and collectivisation, therefore, were made in the early 1950s. There was encouragement from the CPC to peasants to set up mutual-aid teams (groupings of about 10 families) that pooled labour and equipment. Gradually it became apparent to peasants that they could not obtain the tools and equipment that they needed to cultivate their land unless they joined a mutual-aid team but there was as yet no compulsion on them to do so. The communist revolution in the countryside, therefore, was still at an early stage in its development.

Activity

Revision exercise

Using the sources in this section and your own knowledge, explain why it was important for the communist regime to involve the peasants in the process of land reform.

Social reforms

The emancipation of women

In traditional Chinese society, obedience to 'proper' authority, whether in the family or in society at large, was a fundamental duty for all Chinese citizens. For women this meant that as daughters they owed obedience to their fathers, as wives to their husbands and as widows to their eldest sons. Despite the efforts of the Qing emperors to stamp it out, the practice of foot binding of women was widespread by the early 20th century. Arranged marriages, often involving the payment of a dowry, were common. Rich and powerful men kept concubines (mistresses) as well as wives. Before the 20th century, few Chinese women were able to receive any kind of education. The lives of peasant women were particularly harsh. As well as bearing the burden of child rearing and household work, they were expected to labour in the fields and carry on handicraft work at home.

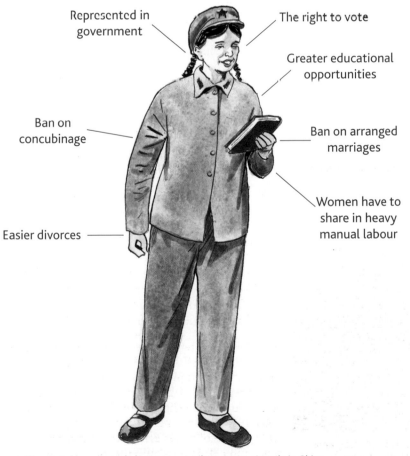

Represented in government · The right to vote · Greater educational opportunities · Ban on concubinage · Ban on arranged marriages · Easier divorces · Women have to share in heavy manual labour

Fig. 3 *Advances made by women under communist rule in China*

My grandmother's feet had been bound when she was two years old. Her mother, who herself had bound feet, first wound a piece of white cloth, about twenty feet long, round her feet, bending all the toes except the big toe inward and under the sole. Then she placed a large stone on top to crush the arch. My grandmother screamed in agony and begged her to stop. Her mother had to stick a cloth into her mouth to gag her. My grandmother passed out repeatedly from the pain. The process lasted several years.

At the age of 15 my grandmother became the concubine of a warlord-general. Wives were not for pleasure – that was what concubines were for. Concubines might acquire considerable power but their social status was quite different from that of a wife. A concubine was a kind of institutionalised mistress, acquired and discarded at will.

4

*From Jung Chang, **Wild Swans**, 1992*

Did you know?

Mao's concubines

Mao himself kept a select group of women around him who, although officially referred to as a PLA dance troupe, were in fact treated as 'imperial concubines' and expected to provide for the Chairman's sexual needs.

The revolution of 1911 had brought some changes for women but not equality. Under the 1912 constitution, women were not granted the right to vote. During the warlord era and beyond, the practice of keeping concubines was widespread, as were arranged marriages. In the growing cities, educated women began to challenge traditional attitudes and make their way in professional occupations. Foot binding gradually began to disappear. However, progress was slow and uneven. In 1922, women accounted for a mere 2.5 per cent of the total numbers of students receiving university education. Under GMD administration, China's cities began to experience social progress with the building of new schools and hospitals and greater opportunities for women. In the countryside, however, social change was slow or non-existent. Foot binding and arranged marriages persisted and there were few educational opportunities for men or women.

The Communists had a better record of promoting equal rights for women. In Jiangxi province in the 1930s, for example, arranged marriages were outlawed and it became illegal to purchase wives. Divorce was made easier. Women were also given the right to vote and Mao stipulated that at least one quarter of those elected to representative bodies had to be women. However, greater equality in many ways increased women's burdens. As the Communists were taking many of the younger men away from the land to fight in the struggle against the GMD, women were expected to do the heavy farm labour that had previously been done by the men as well as continue in their traditional tasks.

After the Communists took power in 1949, one of their first reforms addressed the issue of women's rights. The New Marriage Law 1950 outlawed arranged marriages and the payment of dowries to a husband or his family. Concubinage was banned and unmarried, divorced or widowed women were given the same rights to own property as men. Divorce was made available to

Fig. 4 *Chinese women, bearing weapons, participate in the Long March*

Fig. 5 'The former serf's daughter goes to university.' A propaganda poster illustrating the progress made by women under communist rule

Questions

1. In what ways did women benefit from the communist revolution in China?

2. In what ways had women still not achieved full equality with men?

men and women on equal terms. Attitudes in rural areas were slow to change but the reforms of the early 1950s, together with new educational opportunities, provided a legal and social framework for women to establish equal rights with men.

Improvements in education

Education had traditionally been valued in China as the means to gain entry to the imperial civil service. Entry to schools and universities, however, was severely restricted by the high costs involved, while the heavy demands of the academic curriculum and the very low pass rate in the **imperial examinations** – only 5 per cent of students actually passed in any one year – ensured that this form of education existed solely to produce an elite class of administrators. Western involvement in China during the 19th and 20th centuries had led to the creation of a number of schools and universities offering a Western style of education. By the time of the Communist takeover in 1949 there were 31 schools and universities run by British or American foundations and another 32 run by Christian missionary organisations. In addition, after the revolution of 1911 a growing number of young Chinese took the opportunity to study at Western universities. These educational opportunities promoted the development of an educated professional class in China but for the vast majority of Chinese, particularly the peasants, educational opportunities were virtually non-existent. In the early 20th century, according to one estimate, only 30 per cent of Chinese adults were literate and, before 1949, no more than 20 per cent of Chinese children attended primary school.

In his early writings, Mao had developed his own ideas about education and its role in the building of a socialist society. He rejected the traditional Chinese form of education for its elitism, its old-fashioned curriculum and teaching methods and its reliance on learning from books. For Mao, learning should come from experience. He also opposed Western influence in Chinese schools and universities, which he regarded as a form of **cultural imperialism**. For Mao, education was to play a vital role in the building of a socialist society; economic development required the training of large numbers of skilled specialists,

Key terms

Imperial examinations: China's imperial bureaucracy (civil service) had traditionally been staffed by those who passed rigorous examinations. Candidates for the examinations, who had to stay in special examination compounds for the duration of the tests, had to learn by heart 431,286 characters and five classic texts. These tests, and the curriculum on which they were based, ensured that civil servants learned to conform and did not question the authority of the emperor. The examinations were abolished in 1905 as part of a belated reform programme by the Qing dynasty.

Cultural imperialism: imperialism is normally used to mean the political dominance of one country over another. By 'cultural imperialism' Mao meant that Westerners were using their control over education in China to exercise control over the minds of China's younger generation and to train them in Western ways of thinking.

while political indoctrination could only be achieved through mass literacy. The shortage of educated people in China in 1949 was a serious brake on the future development of the country.

> In our country today there are so many illiterates and yet the building of socialism cannot wait until illiteracy is eliminated; in our country today it is not only the many school-age children who have no schools to go to but also large numbers of young people above that age, to say nothing of adults.
>
> To be a good teacher, one must first be a good pupil. There are many things which cannot be learned from books alone; one must learn from those engaged in production, from the workers, from the peasants, and in schools from the students, from those one teaches.

5   *Mao's views on education. From **Selected Works of Mao Tse-tung***

Emphasis in the early years of communist rule was placed on the development of primary education but progress was slow. By 1956, less than half of children aged between 7 and 16 were in full-time education.

Fig. 6 *'The beams of the red sun illuminate ten thousand generations.' A poster showing an elderly peasant woman telling young children about her sufferings before the Communists came to power*

Some 20 years later, the proportion of primary-age children enrolled in schools had reached 96 per cent. Part of the reason for the slow progress was that the education system was starting from a very low base, particularly in rural areas. However, it was also the case that the new communist government did not make spending on education a high priority. In 1952 the investment by the State in education and culture combined amounted to a mere 6.4 per cent of the total budget.

Education in the new China did not entirely break away from the traditional Chinese model of education. In each district there were so-called 'key schools' to which the best teachers were directed and for which children had to sit a tough entrance examination. In the schools there was a heavy emphasis on testing, examinations and physical education. Although selection was supposed to be based on merit, in practice it was the children of high-ranking party and government officials who occupied most of the places at these schools.

Higher education was expanded and universities were remodelled to concentrate more on technical and scientific subjects, reflecting the country's need for more trained specialists. Large numbers of students were also sent to study at universities in the USSR until the late 1950s. As China became isolated from the West, however, there were no longer any opportunities for Chinese students to study there.

Questions

1 How much progress was made towards improving the educational opportunities for China's citizens in the first 10 years of the communist regime?

2 Explain why progress was slow in these early years.

■ Improvements in public health

Poverty and ignorance were reflected in a complete lack of sanitation, as a result of which fly- and water-borne diseases such as typhoid, cholera, dysentery took a heavy toll. Worm infestation was practically universal, for untreated human and animal manure was the main and essential soil fertiliser. The people lived on the fringe of starvation and this so lowered their resistance to disease that epidemics carried off thousands every year.

6	*A British doctor's assessment of the health of Chinese peasants before 1949*

Before the communist regime took power in 1949, the provision of health care in China was very uneven. In the 19th century, Western-style medicine was first brought to China by missionaries. The efforts of Western churches and charitable foundations resulted in the building of hospitals and, later, medical schools in some of China's largest cities. Under the GMD regime in the 1920s and 1930s, with a growing number of trained doctors, medical care in the cities began to show significant improvements. Chinese medicine, which had a long tradition of treatments using herbs, minerals and acupuncture, was also available but was looked down on by modernisers and discouraged by the GMD regime. The medical needs of those living in rural areas, however, were not addressed by the GMD and the countryside continued to suffer from many endemic diseases and high infant mortality rates.

Activity

Source analysis

Study Figures 7, 8 and 9.

1. Why were posters used to communicate information about public health?

2. What were the political messages of these posters?

Fig. 7 *'Environmental sanitation of city residents', a public health educational poster from 1952 outlining simple practical steps that city dwellers could take for themselves to improve their living conditions*

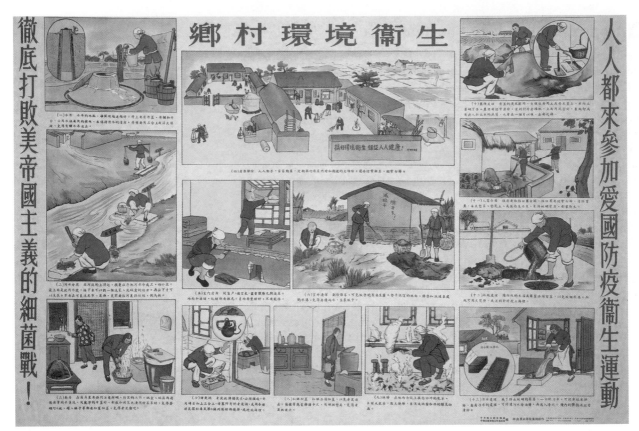

Fig. 8 *'Community sanitation in the countryside', a public health educational poster from 1952 showing the peasants what steps they could take to avoid catching the many diseases that were endemic in the countryside at that time*

Fig. 9 *'Rats, fleas and the plague', a public health educational poster from 1952 showing the link between rats, fleas and disease and the practical steps that could be taken to deal with the problem*

The communist regime placed the emphasis in health care on a preventative rather than a curative approach. This was done largely to compensate for a lack of hospitals and trained doctors. Health reform in the new China mainly took the form of mass campaigns. Using street and neighbourhood committees to mobilise the people, the Communist Party started campaigns such as the Patriotic Health campaign to improve sanitation and hygiene and thereby reduce the incidence of endemic diseases such as cholera, typhoid and scarlet fever. The campaigns produced some improvement as death rates gradually declined. Particular emphasis in these campaigns was placed on improving the quality of drinking water by digging deep wells and on the treatment of human waste. As Source 6 on page 57 shows, the practice of using 'night-soil' as a source of fertiliser for the fields was a major cause of disease in rural areas and efforts were made to encourage peasants to store the waste in pits away from habitation or mix it with chemicals to render it safe.

Sources 7 and 8 show how mass mobilisation of the people was used to improve health.

> We'll get some powdered lime to sprinkle around the drains and damp and shaded places and along the house walls and fences. We've already contracted with a plumber to clean the drains twice a month and we'll share the cost. Besides cleaning up all places where [rats] can nest, we should use traps and bait to catch them. Then we'll send them to the police station. We get credited with every rat we turn into the police.

7   *S. Wood, **A Street in China**, 1958*

Schistosomiasis, a disease that causes internal bleeding, liver damage and a bloating of the abdomen, was common in parts of the Chinese countryside. It was caused by a microscopic worm carried by snails.

> To mobilise the peasantry against the snails it was first necessary to explain to them the nature of the illness which had plagued them for so long, and for this purpose lectures, film shows, posters, radio talks were used. When the peasants came to understand the nature of their enemy, they themselves worked out ways of defeating it.

8   *J. Horn, **Away With All Pests**, 1969*

Workers employed in large industrial enterprises or State enterprises had access to urban hospitals reserved for them. In the rural areas, a three-tier system of health care was adopted. At village level, health care needs were catered for by paramedics working out of village health centres. Each township was to have a health centre providing out-patient care as well as a limited number of beds for in-patient care for less serious cases. The most serious cases were to be referred to county hospitals, which were to be staffed by fully trained doctors. Such facilities were expensive and, with health care taking a mere 1.3 per cent of total State investment in 1952, it was some time before many rural areas saw much improvement.

Questions

1 In what ways were the health and educational systems improved under communist rule?

2 To what extent were there still inequalities in educational opportunities and health care in China by the mid-1950s?

Activity

Preparing a presentation

On your own or in groups, research each of the themes covered in this chapter and present your findings to the class. The focus could be on the extent of change achieved by the Communists in the first five years of their rule.

Learning outcomes

In this section you have looked at the ways in which the Communist Party consolidated its rule in China after 1949. A new system of government was created that established the Communist Party as the leading party in the State. Repression was a key weapon in the struggle against Mao's opponents, from both within and outside the Party. The Communists made many changes to the lives of ordinary Chinese people. The rights of women and access to education were improved, and campaigns were undertaken to improve public health. The communist land reform programme, which had begun in 'liberated areas' in the 1930s, was completed by 1953. After reading this section, you should be able to assess to what extent the lives of women, young people and peasant farmers in particular had changed, and how these changes contributed towards consolidating support for the communist regime.

AQA↗ Examination-style questions

(a) Explain why the communist regime took a cautious approach towards collective ownership of land in the years 1949–53. *(12 marks)*

AQA Examiner's tip
You need to show that you understand what is meant by the words 'cautious approach towards collective ownership' in these years. It would be useful to start by arguing that the ultimate aim of a communist government would be the collective ownership of land but that this was the period when the Communists were trying to consolidate their power and so were moving rather carefully and slowly towards their long-term aims. It would also be worth pointing out that although the Communists had abandoned their earlier caution about confiscating land from landlords, which was shown in some areas during the Civil War, they were careful not to alienate peasants by pushing them towards collective farming too quickly. As with all 'explain why' questions, it is important that you identify and explain a number of factors behind the Communists' decision and that you arrive at a clear and balanced conclusion.

(b) 'Mao's consolidation of power between 1949 and 1953 was entirely dependent on terror and repression.' Explain why you agree or disagree with this view. *(24 marks)*

AQA Examiner's tip
Remember to identify the key words in the quotation before you start to answer this question: in this case, they are 'entirely dependent' and 'terror and repression'. With questions such as this you need to consider points on which you agree with the quotation and points on which you disagree. Make a list of the forms of terror and repression used by the Communists, and then make a list of the other methods they used to consolidate power, such as the ways in which the Communists used reforms to try to win the active support of people. Your answer needs to show balance between agreement and disagreement, although this does not mean that you should not come down on one side or the other. You should aim to produce an answer that has a clear line of argument running through it, that looks at both sides of the debate and that has well selected factual information to support the points being made. Finally, end with a clear conclusion in which you make a judgement.

Economic planning and its results, 1953–67

Controlling the economy

Fig. 1 *'The peasants want freedom but we want socialism'. Mao understood that the peasants wanted the freedom to farm their own plots of land and sell any surplus produce in local markets. Mao's vision of a socialist agriculture involved the peasants' small plots being combined into large collective farms, in which the peasants would work co-operatively to produce more food and the surplus would be shared between them*

In this chapter you will learn about:

- how the Communist Party began the process of collectivising Chinese agriculture

- the beginnings of economic planning and the development of industry

- how the introduction of economic planning led to divisions within the Communist Party

- how Mao dealt with criticism and opposition to his policies.

The collectivisation of agriculture, 1953–7

Mao and the peasants

Mao's long-term aims were to transform China into a socialist society. In terms of what this meant for Chinese agriculture and peasants, he envisaged grouping together small, privately owned farms into much larger, collective farms. This, he believed, would make farms more productive and therefore able to feed China's growing population, and also enable peasants to pool their resources and work together for the common good. However, Mao recognised that China's peasants, having long been exploited by wealthy landlords, wanted nothing more than to have their own small farms and to continue farming in the traditional way. In other words, he recognised that the peasants showed a 'spontaneous tendency towards capitalism'. Needing the support of the peasants in the struggle against the Nationalists during the Civil War, Mao had been careful, despite his long-term aims, to ensure that land confiscated from landlords was redistributed among poorer peasants. Collectivisation would have to wait.

Nikita Krushchev

Nikita Krushchev (1894–1971) was the Soviet leader who succeeded Stalin in 1953. Having spent his early political career serving Stalin, Krushchev made a dramatic secret speech in 1956 in which he denounced Stalin for his cult of personality and for committing crimes during the Great Purges of the 1930s. Krushchev steered Soviet economic and foreign policies in new directions, for which he was denounced by more hard-line communists as a 'revisionist'. He was removed from power in 1964. Mao regarded Krushchev as a revisionist and took to describing opponents within the Chinese Communist Party as the 'Chinese Krushchev'.

The success of Mao's strategy

Mao was nothing if not persistent. If the Party was reluctant to follow him, he became more determined to win the argument, if only because he felt it was necessary for him to assert his authority. In February, he made another speech on the subject of 'On the Correct Handling of Contradictions among the People', in which he repeated his call to 'Let a hundred flowers blossom, let a hundred schools of thought contend.' This time his speech was published to a much wider audience. In the spring of 1957, he embarked on a three-week train journey through eastern China in which he took on the role of a 'wandering lobbyist'. The objects of his attentions were local Party officials, whom he wanted to convince that he was not trying to unleash an uncontrollable tidal wave of criticism. As he had done in the past and would do again in the future, when faced with opposition from one sector of the Party Mao sought allies among other groups. The success of Mao's strategy was evident when, in April 1957, the Politburo sanctioned the campaign.

Fig. 6 *A Chinese propaganda poster*

The campaign begins

With memories of the 1955 purge of intellectuals during the anti-Hu Feng campaign fresh in their minds, most intellectuals were wary of openly criticising the regime. However, when the Hundred Flowers campaign was officially launched in May 1957, it unleashed a torrent of criticisms that attacked the communist system. In the press, magazines, at rallies and on posters, intellectuals attacked the regime for treating the people as their obedient subjects and for developing into a new, privileged, bureaucratic class that was estranged from the people. There were criticisms of abuses of human rights, particularly in the earlier campaigns against counter-revolutionaries, of the slavish following of the Soviet model of development and of the stultifying controls over intellectual life. At Beijing University students created a 'democracy wall' that was covered with posters critical of the Communist Party. There were reports of student riots and strikes and attacks on CPC cadres.

All of this was too much for Mao and the Party hierarchy. By the middle of May, he was attacking 'revisionists' in the Party for working with anti-Party 'rightists' to undermine the regime with their 'wild attacks'.

His attention began to shift from encouraging flowers to bloom to the eradication of 'poisonous weeds'. By early June he was ready to abandon the campaign and in July a full-scale counter-attack on intellectuals was launched. In the ensuing 'anti-rightist' campaign, perhaps as many as 500,000 intellectuals were branded 'rightists' and subjected to varying degrees of persecution. Some were sent to labour camps, others to the countryside for 're-education'. Many intellectuals were driven to suicide by the severe mental pressure to which they were subjected. Although there were many fewer executions than in previous campaigns, there were examples of students and intellectuals being shot in public as a way of terrorising others into submission. As a result of this wave of persecution, independence of thought was systematically crushed; intellectuals in China would never trust Mao or the CPC again.

Mao's motives for starting the Hundred Flowers campaign

Historians have drawn some sharply different conclusions about Mao's motives in launching the Hundred Flowers campaign. For Chang and Halliday, authors of one of the most recent studies of Mao's life, Mao was being devious:

> He cooked up a devious plan. Few guessed that Mao was setting a trap and that he was inviting people to speak out so that he could then use what they said as an excuse to victimise them.

Spence, on the other hand, has argued that the Hundred Flowers campaign was 'not a plot by Mao to reveal the hidden rightists in his country'. He goes on to argue that it was:

> a muddled and inconclusive movement that grew out of conflicts within the Communist Party leadership. At its centre was an argument about the pace and type of development that was best for China.

Short, author of another biography of Mao, has taken another approach. He says that it started as 'an attempt to bridge the gap between the Party and the people'. He also dismisses the idea that Mao was setting a trap and sees his decision to start the campaign as a serious miscalculation. Indeed, Mao:

> made not one but two misjudgements. He underestimated the volume and bitterness of the criticisms, and the Party's ability to withstand them.

Historians generally, therefore, divide into two camps: those who see the Hundred Flowers campaign as a trap set by Mao to expose anti-communist elements among the intellectuals, and those who see the whole episode as a serious error of judgement on Mao's part. To help you understand Mao's decision to start the campaign, you need to consider what he himself said about it.

In 1956, in trying to justify why he wanted to launch a campaign of criticism against the Communist Party, Mao had stated:

> Right now there are certain people who behave as if they can sit back and relax and ride roughshod over the people now that they have the country in their hands. Such people are opposed by the masses, who [want to] throw stones at them and hit them with their hoes. From my point of view, this is what they deserve and I find it most welcome. There are times when nothing but a beating can solve the problem. The Communist Party has to learn its lesson. We must be vigilant, and not allow a bureaucratic lifestyle to develop. We must not form an aristocracy divorced from the people.

6   *Chairman Mao, 1956. From **Selected Works of Mao Tse-tung***

In February 1957 he said:

> Letting a hundred flowers blossom and a hundred schools of thought contend is the policy for promoting progress in the arts and sciences and a flourishing socialist culture in our land. Different forms and styles in art should develop freely and different schools in science should contend freely. Questions of right and wrong in the arts and sciences should be settled through free discussion in artistic and scientific circles, and though practical work in these fields.
>
> We are against poisonous weeds of whatever kind, but we must carefully distinguish between what is really a poisonous weed and what is really a fragrant flower.

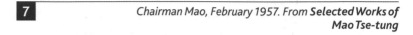

7   *Chairman Mao, February 1957. From* **Selected Works of Mao Tse-tung**

By May 1957, however, Mao's tone had changed completely.

> In recent days the rightists in the democratic parties and institutions of higher education have shown themselves to be most determined and most rabid. We shall let the rightists run amuck for a time and let them reach their climax. The more they run amuck, the better for us. The more outrageous their conduct, the more quickly they will show themselves up as doing the opposite of cooperating with the Communist Party and accepting its leadership. They will then end up by burying themselves.

8   *Chairman Mao, May 1957. From* **Selected Works of Mao Tse-tung**

It is clear from these sources that Mao's policy towards the Hundred Flowers campaign went through many changes during the course of 1956 and 1957. It was entirely consistent with Mao's earlier career that he would seek to unsettle Communist Party officials and counter any tendency that might emerge for them to become bureaucrats, a new 'aristocracy divorced from the people'; the Yan'an Rectification campaign and the Three-Antis campaign were earlier attempts to stop this happening. Although Mao laid some emphasis on the need for free and open debate in the arts and sciences, at the core of the Hundred Flowers campaign was the invitation to non-Party members to criticise aspects of communist rule. When, after overcoming an initial reluctance to speak out, the campaign unleashed a torrent of criticism, Mao's tone changed and he attacked the 'rightists' for going too far and threatening to undermine communist rule. It is entirely possible, as Chang and Halliday have argued, that Mao was prepared for this all along and that he had laid a carefully prepared trap for the unwary to voice their criticisms and so reveal themselves as opponents of the regime. It is also possible that Mao had made a serious miscalculation and that he was covering his tracks by claiming that he had laid a trap in order to justify his mistakes. Mao had shown on a number of occasions in the past that he was a very skilful political operator who could quickly and easily switch from one position to another in order to remain in control of events. For Mao, even if the Hundred Flowers campaign did not develop as he had originally intended, he was able to turn the situation to his advantage and not only remove another swathe of political opponents but also unsettle the Communist Party and hammer home the message once again that only unquestioning obedience to Mao would suffice to ensure survival.

Activity

Source analysis

Study Sources 6, 7 and 8. Summarise the changes in Mao's approach from 1956 to 1957 towards:

- intellectuals
- the Communist Party.

Questions

1   What evidence is there that the Hundred Flowers campaign was a trap set by Mao to expose opposition to Communist rule?

2   What evidence is there that the campaign was a colossal blunder?

3   Using all the evidence give your own assessment of Mao's motives in launching the Hundred Flowers campaign and his later decision to turn it into an anti-rightist campaign.

The consequences of the Hundred Flowers campaign

For many people 1957 was a watershed. My mother was still devoted to the communist cause, but doubts crept in about its practice. She talked about these doubts with her friend, but she never revealed them to my father – not because he had no doubts, but because he would not discuss them with her. Party rules, like military orders, forbade members from talking about Party policies among themselves. It was stipulated in the Party charter that every member must unconditionally obey his Party organisation, that a lower-rank official must obey a higher-rank one. This regimental discipline, which the Communists had insisted on since the Yan'an days and earlier, was crucial to their success. It was a formidable instrument of power, as it needed to be in a society where personal relationships overrode any other rules. My father adhered to this discipline totally. He believed that the revolution could not be preserved and sustained if it were challenged openly. In a revolution you had to fight for your side even if it was not perfect – as long as you believed it was better than the other side. Unity was the categorical imperative.

9
*Jung Chang, **Wild Swans**, 1992*

The treachery of Mao Zedong in repeatedly inviting frank and constructive criticism and then harshly punishing those who gave it completely cowed the Chinese intellectuals so that China's cultural life came to a virtual standstill.

10
*Nien Cheng, **Life and Death in Shanghai**, 1986*

The Hundred Flowers campaign, and the anti-rightist campaign into which it evolved, silenced criticism of the communist regime for a generation. Party unity was strengthened, Mao's position was unchallengeable, but intellectual life in China was stultified. A popular saying of the time was 'After the Three-Antis no one wants to be in charge of money; after the anti-rightist campaign no one opens their mouth.'

Summary questions

1. Explain why Mao showed such suspicion of educated people.
2. Explain why Mao decided to launch the Hundred Flowers campaign in 1957.
3. How successful was the Hundred Flowers campaign for the Communist Party?
4. 'The Hundred Flowers campaign was an important turning point in the history of communist China.' Explain why you agree or disagree with this view.

The Great Leap Forward

In this chapter you will learn about:

■ why in 1958 Mao decided to launch an ambitious economic plan, known as the Great Leap Forward

■ why the Great Leap Forward failed.

Mao called on the nation to increase production of iron and steel to an extraordinarily high level. He raised the slogan 'Catch up with Britain within fifteen years!' All over the city we saw the slogan. The radio relayed the same message. At school, the teachers wrote the slogan on the blackboards. The roads had huge billboards that shouted 'Catch up with Britain within fifteen years!' All public buildings and vehicles displayed it. Shops had it chalked on boards slung from the ceiling. Huge portraits of Chairman Mao looked down on us, with the slogan written underneath. It was everywhere.

I was curious. We Chinese had to catch up with Britain within fifteen years. Britain was the reason I couldn't enjoy my grandmother's wonderful cooking and had to eat the not-so-good food from the canteen. Where, I wondered, was Britain?

 1 From Anhua Gao, ***To the Edge of the Sky***, 2000

Fig. 1 *Mao Zedong takes part in the construction of the Shisanling reservoir in May 1958, during the Great Leap Forward. This photograph reinforces the political message that, under Mao's leadership and guidance, enormous progress could be made through the mass mobilisation of the people*

In January 1958, Mao launched the Great Leap Forward. Under the slogan of 'More, faster, better, cheaper', Mao proclaimed his vision that China could be transformed into a leading industrial power in record time – he believed that it was possible for China to overtake Britain within seven years and the USA soon after. All of this could be achieved through the mass mobilisation of the Chinese people and correct leadership from the Communist Party. It was, of course, a gigantic experiment with far-reaching and potentially devastating consequences for China.

The aims and origins of the Great Leap Forward

Mao's aims

The Great Leap Forward was China's second Five Year Plan. Unlike the first plan, however, the driving force in the effort to achieve production targets for agriculture and industry was not to be a centralised State bureaucracy. Instead, Mao envisaged a decentralisation of control to local Party cadres whose task it would be to mobilise the energies and practical experience of the Chinese people. In this way Mao believed it would be possible for China to achieve rapid and sustained economic growth that would take China very quickly from the stage of Socialism to the stage of fully developed Communism. During 1958, Mao became increasingly caught up in the euphoria of his belief that communist rule could finally unlock China's vast potential and transform the country into the world's leading economic power. In the autumn of 1957, he declared that China would be producing 40 million tonnes of steel by the 1970s, a figure that was twice as high as the one that had been approved by the Central Committee only two months before (and nearly eight times as high as China's actual steel output at the end of the First Five Year Plan). As Mao's confidence grew his expectations were raised even higher; by the autumn of 1958 he was predicting a steel output of 100 million tonnes by 1962 and 700 million tonnes by the early 1970s. As with steel targets, so too with agriculture; in December 1958 he set a target for grain production of 430 million tonnes, more than twice as much as had ever been produced in even the best years.

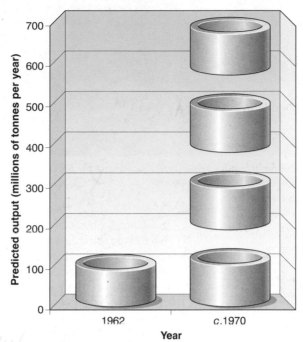

Fig. 2 *Mao's targets for steel production in the Great Leap Forward*

For Mao, the keys to unlocking China's potential were as follows:

■ The grouping of agricultural cooperatives (collective farms) into even larger units known as people's communes. A commune consisted, on average, of about 20,000 people. The communes, once established, became the basic unit of rural society, taking over the functions of local government and becoming military units. Every member of a commune aged between 15 and 50 was a member of the people's militia and the platoons to which they belonged were also the basic work units.

Mao's aim in establishing the communes was to abolish the private, family sphere of peasant life. The peasants' private plots of land were taken over by the commune and all work was organised in a communal, military style. Children were cared for in kindergartens run by the commune (thereby releasing women for manual labour), old people were cared for in communal 'happiness homes' and all meals were provided in mess halls. Family ties were dismissed as 'bourgeois emotional attachments'.

■ Exploring the detail

Communes

The first commune, known as the Sputnik commune, was established in Henan province in April 1958. By the end of the year, 74,000 cooperatives had been grouped into 26,000 communes.

Fig. 3 *Mao Zedong is shown with farmers following his leadership at the time of the Great Leap Forward and the founding of people's communes*

Mao often talked about learning from the peasants' practical experience. In direct contradiction to this policy, however, he drew up an eight-point agricultural constitution based on the discredited theories of the Soviet 'scientist' Lysenko, which farmers were forced to follow in order to increase food production. Among the eight points of this constitution were the instruction to plant crops closer together and to plough the soil much deeper than was normal practice. Both of these policies had disastrous results for grain yields.

■ Under the slogan 'Walking on two legs', communes were ordered to become centres of industrial as well as agricultural production. 'Backyard furnaces' were established to produce iron and steel in communes, schools, colleges and other institutions that had little or no previous experience of iron smelting. Metal implements of all kinds, from cooking pots and cutlery to iron fences, radiators and even locks, were requisitioned to be melted down into pig iron, while wooden furniture, doors and trees were used as fuel.

■ Large-scale civil engineering projects such as bridges, canals and dams were built largely by mobilising tens of thousands of labourers to dig and build by hand rather than using machines.

Exploring the detail

The Four Noes campaign

During the Great Leap Forward, Mao launched the Four Noes campaign to eradicate pests: flies, mosquitoes, rats and sparrows. On the false grounds that sparrows consumed large quantities of seed and grain, people were urged to prevent the birds from landing on the ground or on buildings by keeping up a barrage of noise until the birds dropped dead from exhaustion. The campaign against sparrows was so effective that the ecological balance was upset and caterpillars, on which the birds did actually feed, became more prevalent and consumed large areas of crops.

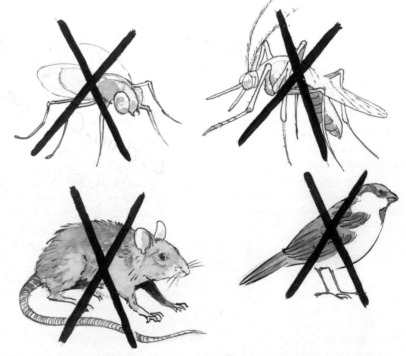
Fig. 4 *The targets of the Four Noes campaign: flies, mosquitos, rats and sparrows*

A huge furnace was erected in the parking lot. At night the sky was lit up, and the noise of the crowds around the furnace could be heard 300 yards away in my room. My family's woks went into the furnace, together with all our cast-iron cooking utensils. We did not suffer from their loss, as we did not need them anymore. No private cooking was allowed now, and everyone had to eat in the canteen. The furnaces were insatiable. Gone was my parents' bed, a soft comfortable one with iron springs. Gone also were the iron railings from the city pavements, and anything else that was iron. I hardly saw my parents for months. They often did not come home at all, they had to make sure that the temperature in their office furnaces never dropped.

2
*From Jung Chang, **Wild Swans**, 1992*

When Mao talked about decentralising the economic planning process and mobilising the energies of China's 600 million people, he was showing once again his frustration with an over-cautious bureaucracy. By 1958 Mao had concluded that Communism in China could be built in a way that ignored the economic realities of the country's development. The economic laws that guided the actions of the professional planners could, in Mao's view, be ignored. The speed with which communes were established and the exaggerated production figures which local officials – anxious to avoid being labelled 'rightists' – reported to the government confirmed Mao in his belief that he had set China on the right course. As his confidence and euphoria grew, so too did the targets that he set. By the end of 1958 Mao's confidence was virtually boundless. For millions of ordinary Chinese, however, Mao's utopian dreams were rapidly becoming a nightmarish struggle for survival.

Factors that influenced Mao's thinking

There were a number of inter-connected factors that lay behind the decision to launch the Great Leap Forward. In order to understand this range of factors, you need to examine the context in which the decisions were made.

The economic context

Despite the successes of Chinese agriculture and industry in achieving most of the targets in the First Five Year Plan, a number of problems had been revealed. Although industrial production overall had risen by 18.7 per cent during the period of the plan, the rise in agricultural production of only 3.8 per cent had been much less impressive. The priority for Mao and the CPC leadership was for industrial growth but, unless Chinese farmers could produce much more food and do so in a more efficient way, industrialisation would be held back. Industrial cities could only expand if there was enough surplus food available to feed a growing urban population, and industrial enterprises could only grow if more peasants could be freed from agricultural labour to work in factories. One possible solution to this problem was the one used by Stalin in the USSR in the 1930s: the forcible requisitioning of food and punitive action against the peasants. With a membership

Activity

Group activity

Draw a diagram to show the political, social, agricultural and industrial aims of the Great Leap Forward. On your diagram, show the links between these various aims.

Fig. 5 *The CPC delegation to the Chinese People's Political Consultative Conference in September 1949. Included in this group are Liu Shaoqi (front row, first from left), Zhou Enlai (middle row, fourth from left) and Chen Yun (back row, second from left)*

■ Cross-reference

See page 49 for more details on **Zhou Enlai**.

For more on **Liu Shaoqi**, see pages 34 and 99–101.

For more on **Deng Xiaoping**, see pages 42 and 99–101.

that was overwhelmingly rural – over 70 per cent of members – this was not an option that the CPC could realistically adopt. Within the CPC leadership in 1957 and early 1958 there was a debate over the best course of action to follow. The cautious approach, favoured by Chen Yun and Zhou Enlai, was to offer peasants material incentives – higher prices and more access to consumer goods – to persuade them to produce and sell more food. This would be underpinned by providing machinery and fertilisers to make farming more productive. A more radical approach was put forward by Mao and supported by Deng Xiaoping and Liu Shaoqi. This involved a propaganda campaign to encourage the peasants to work harder and the mass mobilisation of peasant labour through the communes.

■ Key profile

Chen Yun

Originally a worker from Shanghai, Chen Yun (1900–95) joined the CPC in 1924 and rose to become a member of the Politburo in 1934. His specialist knowledge was in economics.

Fig. 6 *Mao Zedong on a visit to a steel works in Hefei, October 1959. This was part of Mao's efforts to boost support for the Great Leap Forward*

The political context

Mao was the instigator and driving force behind the Great Leap Forward. As undisputed leader of the CPC, he had become accustomed to imposing his will on the Party and the Party had become accustomed to giving way. The experience of the Hundred Flowers campaign and the subsequent anti-rightist campaign had not only intimidated China's intellectuals, the CPC at all levels had been unnerved as well. Therefore, although favouring a more cautious approach, not for the first time Zhou Enlai fell into line with Mao's wishes over the Great Leap Forward and was even obliged to make a self-criticism for his past 'right conservatist' errors. If someone of the stature of Zhou Enlai could not oppose Mao over this hair-brained leap into the unknown, then lower-level Party officials had also learned that their own survival depended on telling Mao what he wanted to hear. Mao's regime lacked any checks and balances. There was nobody with the courage or the authority to stand up to him and ensure that the Party followed a policy based on reasoned argument.

Rivalries within the CPC leadership also played their part in the story of the Great Leap Forward. In February 1958, responsibility for the oversight of economic planning was transferred from the State bureaucracy of the PRC to the Communist Party. Therefore, Deng Xiaoping and Liu Shaoqi, both leading figures within the Party, gained at the expense of Zhou Enlai and Chen Yun whose power lay within the central government. At a local level, Party cadres took over from technical experts as the driving force behind increased production. This reflected the priorities of the Great Leap Forward – technical expertise, which in any case was distrusted by Mao, was regarded as a block on development. For Mao, it was more important to be 'red' than to be an expert; in other words, political objectives were more important than economic ones.

The international context

The launch of *Sputnik*, the first satellite, into space by the USSR in October 1957 excited admiration around the world. For Mao this demonstrated the superiority of Soviet technology and the social system on which it was based, and buoyed his growing optimism. It was no accident that the first commune in China, established in Henan province in April 1958, was named the Sputnik commune.

However, despite admiration for Soviet technology, there were growing strains in the relationship between the PRC and the USSR. When Mao declared the formation of the PRC in October 1949, he said that the Chinese people had 'stood up' and that a century of foreign aggression towards China had finally come to an end. In the early years of the republic, Mao accepted 'fraternal' assistance from the USSR in the form of technical assistance and loans, but the Chinese nationalist in Mao always found this dependence on a foreign power humiliating. Moreover, by 1957 and in the light of the experience of the First Five Year Plan, there was a growing feeling among the CPC leadership that the Soviet model of development was not appropriate for China. What Mao was looking for was a specifically Chinese solution to the problem of rapid industrialisation. Communes seemed to provide the solution he was looking for.

Mao wanted China to become a great power, armed with nuclear weapons and capable of regaining control of Taiwan – something that would certainly bring a clash with the USA. In a secret agreement between China and the USSR in 1957, the Soviet leader Khrushchev promised to give China access to nuclear weapons technology. At the same time, however, he began to expound the doctrine of 'peaceful coexistence' with the West, a policy that placed a high priority on improving relations with the USA. For Mao this was a betrayal of international socialist solidarity. Mao became increasingly convinced that China would have to stand alone in its efforts to develop its economy and achieve great power status. The Great Leap Forward was, in part, an assertion by Mao of Chinese independence from the USSR.

The ideological context

A recurring theme in Mao's career was his fear that the Chinese communist revolution was in danger of losing its vitality and becoming bogged down in bureaucratic administration. For Mao, the crucial reference point was the time spent in Yan'an in the 1930s and 1940s. This was seen as a period when the Communist Party had been closest to the masses, when its revolutionary fervour had not yet been tarnished with 'bureaucratism', and when the Party had, by mobilising the mass of the peasants, been able not merely to survive against overwhelming odds but eventually to conquer its enemies. Mao frequently harked back to the Yan'an experience for inspiration and direction and he did so again in 1957 and 1958.

As Chairman of the Party, Mao was removed from the day-to-day business of government and policy making. His way of asserting himself was to stress the importance of ideology, an area which he had made his own sphere. In the context of the Great Leap Forward, three aspects of his ideology were particularly relevant:

■ His view that, through political will and mass mobilisation, economic laws ignored and material conditions overcome. In 1958, Mao believed that, with correct political leadership and application of technology, China's 600 million people could be mobilised to overcome their existing poverty and scarcity and make a 'great leap forward' into prosperity and plenty.

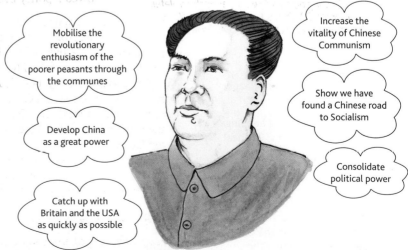

Mobilise the revolutionary enthusiasm of the poorer peasants through the communes

Develop China as a great power

Catch up with Britain and the USA as quickly as possible

Increase the vitality of Chinese Communism

Show we have found a Chinese road to Socialism

Consolidate political power

Fig. 7 *Mao's aims for the Great Leap Forward*

■ Linked to his belief in the power of human will, Mao also developed his thoughts on the concept of 'continuing revolution'.

■ Mao had long believed that the peasants were the most revolutionary class in China and that the key to China's economic and political development lay in the countryside. The emphasis on rural communes in the Great Leap Forward reflected Mao's determination to prove that the peasantry could lead the drive towards a communist future.

> Our revolutions come one after another. Starting from the seizure of power in the whole country in 1949, there followed in quick succession the anti-feudal land reform, the agricultural co-operativisation, and the socialist reconstruction of private industries, commerce and handicrafts. Now we must start a technological revolution so that we may overtake Britain in fifteen or more years. After fifteen years, when our foodstuffs and iron and steel have become more plentiful, we shall take a much greater initiative. Our revolutions are like battles. After a victory, we must at once put forward a new task. In this way, cadres and the masses will forever be filled with revolutionary fervour, instead of conceit.

3 *Chairman Mao, January 1958. From **Selected Works of Mao Tse-tung***

The Great Leap Forward was, for Mao, another stage in China's 'continuing revolution', using methods that had seemingly been used effectively before in Yan'an and elsewhere. In official statements from the Party Central Committee and Mao himself, the impetus for the move towards large communes had come from the peasants themselves. In late 1957 in some areas millions of peasants had been mobilised to undertake large-scale projects in water conservation and irrigation. Because men were taken away from the fields to undertake this work, women took their places. This led to the establishment of communal organisations for feeding and childcare. So the idea of communes was born, although in reality it was enthusiastic local CPC cadres who had been behind the creation of the first communes. Nevertheless this confirmed in Mao his belief that 'Poor people want change, want to do things, want revolution.' A four-month tour of China's provinces in early 1958, in which he sought 'truth from facts', further reinforced his view that communes were an essential part of Chinese revolutionary ideology. In reality, what he learned on his tour was only what the local Party cadres wanted him to hear. Nevertheless, convinced that he was better informed and more ideologically correct than the more cautious members of the Politburo, he was able to override their doubts and set increasingly radical and unrealistic targets for the Great Leap Forward.

Fig. 8 *A painting showing irrigation of crops by Chinese farmers*

Activity

Revision exercise

1 Divide a large sheet of paper into four quarters.

2 Write the following headings in the four sections: Political context; Economic context; International context; Ideological context.

3 Summarise the main factors that influenced Mao's thinking on the Great Leap Forward under the appropriate headings.

■ Why did the Great Leap Forward fail?

> During this past year, there have been so many good things. Trails have been blazed. Many things have been realised, about which we did not even dare to dream before.

4 *Chairman Mao, December 1958. From **Selected Works of Mao Tse-tung***

The optimism and euphoria that had created the over-inflated targets of the Great Leap Forward did not survive long after Mao had made the statement in Source 4. In 1958, there had been a good harvest, mainly due to favourable weather conditions, but the amount of grain produced fell a long way short of the claims made by the government. An all-time record harvest of 375 million tonnes of grain was trumpeted by the government as proof that the Great Leap Forward had been a resounding success. The actual figure was nearer to 200 million tonnes. Nevertheless, Mao used the published figure as evidence that his policies were working and set an even more fantastic figure – 430 million tonnes – as the target for 1959. The harvest in 1959, however, was the worst for many years. The government declared a harvest of 270 million tonnes but the actual figure was nearer to 170 million tonnes. In 1960, the situation deteriorated still further, with only 143 million tonnes of grain being produced. By the summer of 1959, food shortages began to hit the cities; rice rations were reduced and vegetables and cooking oil disappeared completely.

In steel production the same pattern of apparent early successes followed by catastrophic failure was repeated. The establishment of backyard furnaces was achieved with astonishing speed. In September 1958, 14 per cent of steel was produced in such furnaces; a month later the figure had increased to 49 per cent. At the peak of the campaign to produce steel in this way, some 90 million people were involved. The results, however, fell a long way short of expectations. Only 9 million tonnes of steel (later revised to 8 million tonnes) of acceptable quality were produced in 1958. The targets for later years were revised downwards but were still set at impossibly high levels. For 1959, the target was 20 million tonnes and, for 1962, 60 million tonnes. Needless to say, none of these targets were met. Moreover, the quality of steel produced in the backyard furnaces was very poor and much of it was left to rust. In the spring of 1959 the experiment with backyard furnaces was abandoned.

Failure of the Great Leap Forward was guaranteed. A project based on the total denial of the actual capacity of China's agricultural and industrial base, a refusal to be bound by economic laws and an assertion that economic targets could be based on political necessity rather than rational calculation was bound to fail. There were, however, a number of specific factors that contributed to the failure:

- Weather conditions in 1959 made the situation worse. Floods in the south of China and a drought in the north (which continued into 1960) significantly reduced the harvest.

- The anti-rightist campaign of 1957 had resulted in the purge of many crucial experts, particularly the statisticians who had been responsible for collecting and analysing production figures during the First Five Year Plan. This campaign had also seriously unnerved Party cadres at all levels and led them to conclude that their survival depended on telling Mao what he wanted to hear. Reports of production figures from the communes were seriously inflated and this contributed to the atmosphere of euphoria in the early stages of the Great Leap Forward.

- The Great Leap Forward involved a monumental waste of both human and material resources. This was largely due to the competing demands that were placed on the communes. Frequent military training took peasants away from their work. Work teams were often too busy trying to fulfil their steel targets to work in the fields; the result was that ripened grain was often left to rot because there was no one available to harvest it. Melting down farm implements to make steel left the peasants with too few tools with which to cultivate the land. On many communes land was actually left uncultivated because it was assumed that so much food would be grown using the new methods that there would not be enough granary space to store it.

- The break with the USSR in 1960 led to the withdrawal of thousands of Soviet experts who had been helping the Chinese to develop their economy through planning. The Soviet Union also stopped making

Activity
Challenge your thinking

'For Mao, political considerations were always more important than economic development.' Explain why you agree or disagree with this statement.

Exploring the detail

Propaganda

As propaganda replaced accurate information during the Great Leap Forward, reports of an abundance of food actually encouraged peasants to consume more and waste more. The regime became the victim of its own propaganda, but it was the Chinese people who paid the price.

Activity

Thinking point

In what ways did the failure of the Great Leap Forward reveal serious weaknesses in the communist regime?

Exploring the detail

Mao's misconceptions

The Great Leap Forward was based on poor science. The concept of planting crops close together, championed by Mao, exhausted the soil and actually reduced yields in later years. Deep ploughing contributed to soil erosion, as did cutting down forests to provide fuel for the backyard furnaces.

loans to the PRC to help finance economic growth. However, as the Great Leap Forward was already failing before the Soviet Union withdrew its help, this was not a major cause of the failure. On the other hand, previous dependence on the Soviet Union for technical expertise and heavy machinery still had to be paid for; even though food was in desperately short supply in China, millions of tonnes of grain continued to be exported to the USSR to repay earlier loans.

■ Mao had over-estimated the revolutionary enthusiasm of the Chinese people. Many peasants were reluctant to pool their resources and slaughtered their animals rather than hand them over to the communes. There were instances of peasants hoarding grain for their own consumption. In previous land reforms, the CPC had been careful to win the active cooperation of the peasants and to proceed cautiously when it was clear that the peasants were reluctant to give up their private plots. During the Great Leap Forward, however, political pressure and compulsion drove the process of forming communes. Far from this being the result of a spontaneous movement by the peasants themselves, enthusiastic local CPC cadres, taking their lead from Mao, forced the pace of change. When it became clear that many communes had been set up without adequate preparation and were not working effectively, Mao blamed over-zealous local cadres for the failure and tried to restrain some of

Fig. 9 *Liu Shaoqi and Mao Zedong together in April 1959*

the more enthusiastic local leaders. This failure of the political system, however, was Mao's own responsibility. Regional and local officials took their lead from him. The anti-rightist campaign had ensured that no Party cadre would dare question the direction of Party policy or the official claims of success. The Great Leap Forward was launched and driven forward at Mao's insistence: its failure was primarily due to him.

Summary questions

1. Explain why Mao decided to launch the Great Leap Forward.
2. 'In launching the Great Leap Forward, Mao was pursuing political objectives.' Explain why you agree or disagree with this view.
3. How successful was the Great Leap Forward?
4. Explain why the Great Leap Forward failed to achieve its objectives.

7 The aftermath of the Great Leap Forward

Fig. 1 *Mao Zedong on the Lushan mountain in 1961. When this photograph was taken, the famine which resulted in the loss of millions of lives was at its height*

In this chapter you will learn about:

- the results of the Great Leap Forward for the Chinese people

- how far the failure of the Great Leap Forward weakened Mao's position

- how this failure caused divisions within the Communist Party over the future direction of economic planning

- the growing power struggle within the Communist Party.

The setting up of rural people's communes throughout the countryside in 1958 radically changed the situation. For the first time in China's history, large-scale collectivisation created the political, social and economic conditions which could support a rural system of social security and welfare services.

Then came three bad years during which, chiefly because of exceptionally widespread drought and floods, poor harvests were reaped throughout the country. During these three years the people were short of food, but none starved. When the lean years passed, the whole nation realised the truth of what Chairman Mao had been saying for years – that agriculture was and must be the foundation of the national economy.

1   *From J. Horn, **Away With All Pests**, 1969*

The results of the Great Leap Forward

Joseph Horn, the author of Source 1, was a British doctor who had gone to live and work in China in the 1950s and was therefore able to witness the Great Leap Forward at first hand. As Source 1 shows, he was a supporter of the regime. Jung Chang, the daughter of a communist official, also witnessed the effects of the Great Leap Forward at close quarters.

Activity

Source analysis

Study Sources 1 and 2. Explain why two people, both of whom lived in China at the time of the Great Leap Forward, could give such contrasting accounts of its effects.

Starvation was much worse in the countryside because there were no guaranteed rations. Government policy was to provide food for the cities first, and commune officials were having to seize grain from the peasants by force. In many areas, peasants who tried to hide food were arrested, or beaten and tortured. Commune officials who were reluctant to take food from the hungry peasants were themselves dismissed, and some were physically maltreated. As a result, the peasants who had actually grown the food died in their millions all over China.

| 2 | *From Jung Chang, **Wild Swans**, 1992* |

Fig. 2 *Requisitioning food from the peasants made the famine worse and caused millions of deaths*

Joseph Horn's account reflects the official 1960s Chinese version of the effects of the Great Leap Forward on the Chinese people. It was not until 1980 that Hu Yaobang, the General Secretary of the CPC, officially acknowledged that there had indeed been a famine in the years 1959–62 and that 20 million people had died as a result. Since then, a number of studies by Western and Chinese historians have produced wide variations in the estimates of how many people died.

The result was famine on a gigantic scale, a famine that claimed 20 million lives or more between 1959 and 1962. Many others died shortly thereafter from the effects of the Great Leap – especially children, weakened by years of progressive malnutrition.

| 3 | *From J. D. Spence, **The Search for Modern China**, 1990* |

In 1959 and 1960, some 20 million Chinese starved to death and 15 million fewer children were born, because women were too weak to conceive. Five million more perished from hunger in 1961. It was the worst human disaster ever to befall China.

| 4 | *From P. Short, **Mao: A Life**, 1999* |

Close to 38 million died of starvation and overwork in the Great Leap Forward and the famine which lasted four years. This was the greatest famine of the twentieth century – and of all recorded human history. Mao knowingly starved and worked these tens of millions of people to death. During the two critical years, 1958–9, grain exports alone, almost exactly 7 million tons, would have provided the equivalent of over 840 calories per day for 38 million people – the difference between life and death.

| 5 | From Jung Chang and J. Halliday, **Mao: The Unknown Story**, 2006 |

Activity

Source analysis

Study Sources 3, 4 and 5. Why can historians not agree on the numbers who died during the famine?

It would have been difficult to count the numbers of deaths from this famine in a country the size of China. Mao's regime at the time did not even try because it denied that there was a famine at all. Subsequent attempts to estimate the numbers who died have used different methodologies. Those who have arrived at a figure of around 20 million deaths have calculated the numbers of 'excess deaths', i.e. people who died in addition to the numbers who would have died in normal years. Higher figures have been obtained by taking the figures for the worst hit areas of China and extrapolating them to the country as a whole. This method is not entirely reliable as it is known that the famine was worse in some areas than in others. What can be said with some certainty is that the Great Leap Forward caused a disaster on an unprecedented scale and that tens of millions of Chinese suffered its effects for years to come. The famine was worst in rural areas than in cities and some regions suffered more than others. It has been estimated that one fifth of the population of Xizang (Tibet) was wiped out in the famine. In Anhui, Henan and Sichuan, where enthusiastic provincial Party secretaries had promoted the Great Leap Forward most strongly, perhaps as many as one quarter of the population died. Even in Beijing, which was the best supplied city, the annual death rate increased by 250 per cent during the famine years. Prostitution and banditry, which had been all but stamped out in the early years of the communist regime, began to reappear. In Henan, the militia units that had been established for self-defence during the Great Leap Forward committed the worst crimes of armed robbery, rape and murder. In Sichuan, Xizang and other Western provinces, the PLA had to be deployed to put down armed rebellions among the peasants. Worst of all, there were reports from some areas of people turning to cannibalism. The labour camps were expanded to accommodate the many peasants found guilty of trying to cultivate food for themselves or hiding food destined to be requisitioned by the government for city dwellers.

That winter [1960] cannibalism became common. Generally the villagers ate the flesh of corpses, especially those of children. In rare cases, parents ate their own children, elder brothers ate younger brothers, elder sisters ate their younger sisters. In most cases, cannibalism was not punished by the Public Security Bureaux because it was not considered as severe a crime as destroying State property and the means of production. This latter crime often merited the death sentence. Travelling around the region [Henan] over thirty years later, every peasant that I met over 50 said he personally knew of a case of cannibalism in his production team.

| 6 | J. Becker, **Hungry Ghosts**, 1996 |

Exploring the detail

The effects of famine

During the famine of the late 1950s there were reports of people eating tree bark and grass to find some nourishment. In a situation where people were desperate for food, social order began to break down. Parents sold their children and husbands sold their wives in return for food.

Activity

Source analysis

Study Source 6. What can we learn from this about the effects of the famine on the peasants in Henan?

■ Exploring the detail

China's space programme

In 1960, China's first rocket, based on a Soviet design, was tested for the first time. After the break with the Soviet Union, China continued to develop its space and rocket programme but Chinese scientists started to design their own rockets. In 1964, this resulted in the launch of China's first ballistic missile, the *Dangfeng* rocket.

■ Exploring the detail

Peng's visit

In 1959, Peng Dehuai returned to his native village of Niaoshi where he saw lumps of useless pig iron rusting in the fields and the houses stripped of timber to fuel the furnaces. In the so-called 'happiness homes', elderly people were thin and frail and had no blankets to keep them warm. Peng did not speak out immediately against the failures of the Great Leap Forward, as he was well aware of the dangers facing those who openly criticised Mao. Mao, for his part, was already suspicious of Peng's ideological purity because, as Defence Minister, he had been responsible for making the PLA into a more professional, but less egalitarian, organisation.

By the early 1960s the Chinese government was having to import food, a policy that ran completely counter to the self-reliance that the Great Leap Forward was supposed to have achieved. In 1961, 6 million tonnes of wheat were imported, mainly from Canada and Australia but also, indirectly, from the USA. Imports continued at this level until the 1970s. It is difficult to find many positive achievements that came out of the Great Leap Forward. Mass mobilisation of labour on large-scale irrigation projects did bring the possibility of development to previously infertile regions. The capital city, Beijing, experienced a radical redevelopment that resulted in the destruction of the old city walls and the building of wider boulevards. The monumental Tiananmen Square was also created in this period. China began to develop its own nuclear weapons which resulted, in 1964, in the testing of its first atomic bomb. When set against the cost in human lives, however, these achievements pale into insignificance.

■ The Third Five Year Plan and debates about economic policy

The purge of Peng Dehuai

In December 1958, Mao stepped down as Chairman (Head of State) of the PRC. He had spoken a number of times previously about his wish to retire to the 'second front' and this was his way of doing so. He was replaced by Liu Shaoqi. This did not mean, however, that Mao was in any way relinquishing his power. He still retained his positions of Chairman of the CPC and Chairman of the Military Affairs Commission (MAC). He was merely relieving himself of the day-to-day duties of the Head of State and giving himself more time and space to concentrate on ideological matters, on which his authority was supreme.

When Mao launched the Great Leap Forward in 1958, it was clear that not all of the senior members of the Communist Party shared his optimism and his belief in the power of mass mobilisation. However, none of the Politburo were prepared to openly challenge him. In 1959, as it began to appear that the propagandist claims of unparalleled success in the Great Leap Forward did, in fact, mask a developing disaster, Mao faced his first serious challenge. Earlier in the year Peng Dehuai had returned to his birthplace in Henan and learned at first hand from the peasants about the real effects of the Great Leap Forward. Serious food shortages had already begun to appear and Peng found the people in a mood of rebellion against communal life and highly critical of the waste that resulted from Party policies. As minister of defence, Peng also knew that military transport was already being used to take relief food to the worst-hit areas.

At the next meeting of the Central Committee of the Party, at Lushun in July 1959, Peng tried to meet Mao to express his concerns. As Mao was not available, Peng decided to put his views in writing in a 'letter of opinion' – something he was perfectly entitled to do as a senior member of the Politburo. In his letter he praised the overall achievements of the Great Leap Forward but criticised specific failings. In other words, he argued that the policy was correct in theory but flawed in practice. In apportioning responsibility for the failures, he did not exempt Mao from criticism. What had been intended as a private letter addressed to Mao alone was published by Mao to all the delegates and used as an opportunity to destroy Peng's career. Peng had impeccable credentials as a Communist and veteran of the revolutionary struggle. He had a reputation for being incorruptible and independent-minded. He also had a long history of disagreements with Mao but his reputation and status within the communist hierarchy were not enough to save him from Mao's determination to destroy him.

In his response to Peng's letter, Mao charged him with having deviated from the Party's 'general line' – one of the worst crimes of which a leading Communist could be accused. Peng was denounced as a 'rightist', like so many before him. Mao went on to say that criticism of the Party could lead to the collapse of its power and in those circumstances he would 'go away to the countryside, to lead the peasants and overthrow the government'. After the

Fig. 3 *Defence Minister Peng Dehuai reports on the Korean War, 1953*

Central Committee meeting, Mao convened a meeting of the Politburo to decide Peng's fate. It was unfortunate for Peng that his criticisms of the Great Leap Forward seemed to echo those of the Soviet leadership at a time of rapidly worsening relations with the USSR. Peng was accused of 'objectively aiding China's enemies' and leading a 'right-opportunist anti-Party clique'. Having been found guilty of all charges, Peng was dismissed as Defence Minister and placed under virtual house arrest. Although he retained his place on the Politburo, he never attended another meeting. His career was finished. To replace him as Defence Minister, Mao brought Lin Biao out of semi-retirement.

The Peng Dehuai affair was another defining moment in the history of the Chinese Communist Party. Before this it had been assumed that any leading comrade could express his views freely at Party meetings as long as the final decision was accepted by all. After Lushun, it was no longer safe for leading Communists to air views that were critical of Mao. The event had other repercussions. In 1959, there had been signs that Mao was beginning to moderate some of the wilder aspects of the Great Leap Forward. After Lushun, in a gesture seemingly designed to prove that Mao had been correct all along, he swung to the left again and launched the second Great Leap Forward in 1959–60. Therefore, an opportunity had been lost to correct a failing policy and the resulting disaster was even greater than it might otherwise have been. Finally, in an effort to root out any wider opposition within the CPC, yet another purge was launched against Party members and low-level officials. Some 6 million people were subjected to struggle meetings and forced to make self-criticism. In Sichuan alone, 80 per cent of the basic-level cadres were dismissed from the Party.

The Third Five Year Plan

By 1961 there were signs that the Communist Party leadership were beginning to rethink their flawed economic policies. In April 1961, the communal canteens were abandoned and peasants were once again allowed to feed themselves at home – not that there was much food with which to do so. By June 1961 peasants were allowed to cultivate their own private plots and the communes began to introduce financial incentives to encourage peasants to work harder. Rural fairs and markets were again permitted and gradually many of the communes were broken up into smaller units based on single villages. By 1962 the retreat from the Great Leap Forward had gone even further. Some 25 million peasants who had drifted to the towns in search of work and food were returned to their home villages. Around 25,000 inefficient enterprises set up under

Cross-reference

Struggle meetings are covered in more detail on page 38.

Activity

Revision exercise

1 Summarise Mao's reasons for purging Peng Dehuai.

2 Compare the treatment of Peng Dehuai with the treatment of Gao Gang and Rao Shushi in the earlier purge of 1953 (Chapter 3).

   a What features did the two purges have in common?

   b What features were different?

the Great Leap had been closed down. Coal and steel targets had been reduced to more realistic levels and industrial workers were once again offered financial incentives to increase production.

There was also a brief but significant period of political liberalisation. Zhou Enlai and Liu Shaoqi led the way in rehabilitating many of the 'rightists' purged in 1957–8. Vice-Premier Chen Yi even went as far as to say that 'China needs intellectuals, needs scientists. For all these years they have been unfairly treated. They should be restored to the position they deserve.' Mao did not obstruct this policy but he did not wholeheartedly approve of it either.

This new, pragmatic approach to economic planning was largely the work of Chen Yun, one of the leading economic planners within the CPC hierarchy. In 1961, Chen had visited a commune near Shanghai and learned at first hand from the peasants about their grievances and their suggestions for improving production. It was Chen Yun who was mainly responsible for drawing up the Third Five Year Plan, launched in 1962. In this new phase of economic planning there was a significant shift away from the priorities and methods of the Great Leap Forward. Central bureaucratic control replaced the decentralisation of planning to the communes. Experts and their technical knowledge were once again valued. Production targets were reviewed on an annual basis, making the whole system more flexible. Finally, the reintroduction of financial incentives to encourage workers and peasants to work harder took the place of the moral exhortations and appeals to revolutionary fervour that had characterised the Great Leap. This more pragmatic approach gradually began to show results. By 1965 agricultural production was back to the levels attained in 1957. The output of light industry expanded by 27 per cent while that of heavy industry increased by 17 per cent. More dramatically, oil production increased by 1,000 per cent and natural gas by 4,000 per cent, freeing China from its dependence on the USSR for energy supplies.

Debates about economic policy

Mao on the defensive

Despite his success in crushing Peng Dehuai and silencing criticism of the Great Leap Forward, Mao's prestige suffered from the catastrophic failure of his policies. Chen Yun's more pragmatic approach to the Third Five Year Plan and economic recovery was supported by Deng Xiaoping, Liu Shaoqi and Bo Yibo, although Mao showed himself to be increasingly appalled by what he regarded as a retreat into **'revisionism'**. In January 1962, a 7,000-cadre conference was called by Mao in a bid to rally support against any further drift away from his socialist ideals. The results of the conference, however, were not as Mao had intended. In a key speech to the conference, Liu Shaoqi praised Mao for his correct leadership but then went on to say 'It is necessary to point out that the primary responsibility for the shortcomings and errors in our work in these past few years lies with the Party centre.' The 'Party centre' included Mao, Liu himself and the rest of the Politburo, so Liu was clearly implying that Mao must share part of the

> ■ **Key term**
>
> **Revisionism**: a term used by Marx to describe Socialists who modified or 'revised' his theories. The worst form of revisionism from Marx's point of view was the argument that Socialism could be achieved by peaceful, non-revolutionary means. Mao often used this term to describe opposition to his policies. He also used the term to describe Krushchev's policies in the USSR.

Fig. 4 *Mao Zedong meets Liu Shaoqi (left) and Chen Yun (centre) in January 1961*

blame for past mistakes. Mao was caught unawares by this speech and judged that the mood of the conference was supportive of Liu's speech. Later in the conference Mao made a form of self-criticism in which he accepted responsibility as Chairman but made no apology or admission of personal mistakes. Nevertheless, the effect was highly significant. A figure who had previously enjoyed an aura of infallibility was, for the first time, admitting to failings. Moreover, Mao left the meeting with a feeling that his warnings about the dangers of revisionism had not been heeded by the delegates. For the next few months he withdrew from public life, leaving Liu Shaoqi, Deng Xiaoping (CPC General Secretary) and Zhou Enlai (Prime Minister) in charge of the Party and the State.

> Any mistakes that the centre has made ought to be my direct responsibility, and I also have an indirect share of the blame because I am Chairman of the Central Committee. I don't want other people to shirk their responsibility. There are some other comrades who also bear responsibility, but the person primarily responsible should be me.

7   *Chairman Mao, 1962. From* **Selected Works of Mao Tse-tung**

Activity

Source analysis

Study Source 7. To what extent does this source show that Mao was making a genuine admission of error and responsibility for his part in the Great Leap Forward?

Ideological differences

Gradually a clear ideological divide was beginning to appear between Mao and Liu Shaoqi and Deng Xiaoping. The pragmatism of Liu and Deng can perhaps best be summed up by a statement made by Deng in June 1962. 'It doesn't matter', Deng argued, 'if the cat is black or white; so long as it catches the mouse, it is a good cat.' In other words, Deng was saying that the real test of a policy's value is whether it works and achieves results, not whether it is ideologically correct. In the eyes of Liu, Deng and Chen Yun, the situation facing China was so desperate at the end of the Great Leap Forward that the main priority must be to put the country back on its feet, even if this meant making ideological compromises such as restoring some element of private farming and private trade. Liu also favoured adopting a more conciliatory stance towards the USA and the USSR as China needed to avoid confrontations with other powers at a time when its own economy was in crisis. They believed that mass mobilisation was not an effective approach to economic development; rather, control of the economy should be placed in the hands of technical experts.

Mao on the offensive

To Mao this was all dangerous heresy. In his view China was, by 1962, recovering quickly from the failures of the Great Leap and no further retreats from socialist ideals were necessary. Indeed, his priority was always ideological purity. Although he conceded that mass mobilisation had not succeeded in achieving rapid economic development, this was no longer his main concern. He retained his faith in mass mobilisation as a means of class struggle, through which the gains of the revolution would be protected and socialist ideals preserved. Mao's aim was to revive the revolutionary fervour of the masses and to struggle against bureaucratic control over the economy and the danger that a bourgeoisie might emerge within the Party. At the annual summer conference in 1962, Mao returned to the political fray and posed a stark choice for China's leaders: 'Are we going to take the socialist road or the capitalist road? Do we want rural cooperation or don't we?' In his view the line being taken by Liu and Deng was 'Chinese revisionism', which had to be combated. 'Oppose revisionism (abroad), prevent revisionism (at home)' was the simple slogan that Mao used to rally the Party against the policies of Liu and Deng.

Activity

Thinking point

Summarise the main ideological differences between Mao and the State economic planners (Chen Yun, Liu Shaoqi and Deng Xiaoping).

In our country we must admit the possibility of the restoration of reactionary classes. We must raise our vigilance and properly educate our youth, otherwise a country like ours may yet move towards its opposite. Therefore, from now on, we must talk about this every year, every month, every day, so that we have a more enlightened Marxist-Leninist line on the problem.

8   *Chairman Mao, May 1962. From **Selected Works of Mao Tse-tung***

If things were allowed to go on this way, the day would not be too far off – a few years, over ten years, or a few decades at the most – when the resurgence of a nationwide counter-revolution became inevitable, It would then be a certainty that the Party of Marxism-Leninism would turn into a party of revisionism, of fascism. The whole of China would then change colour. The Socialist Education Movement is a struggle that calls for the re-education of man and for a confrontation with the forces of feudalism and capitalism that are now feverishly attacking us. We must nip their counter-revolution in the bud.

9   *Chairman Mao, May 1963. From **Selected Works of Mao Tse-tung***

Activity

Source analysis

Study Sources 8 and 9. What can we learn from these sources about Mao's priorities in the aftermath of the failure of the Great Leap Forward?

Exploring the detail

The Socialist Education Movement

This was intended to be a comprehensive programme to reintroduce basic socialist values into Chinese society. Class struggle was re-emphasised in a campaign for the 'four clean-ups' – to remove corruption in the countryside relating to accounting procedures, grain supplies and property accumulation and in the system of allocating work points to peasants for their labour. Thousands of cadres were relocated to the countryside, both to learn from the peasants and to boost the Party's propaganda efforts among them.

Cross-reference

See Chapter 8 for the climax of this power struggle, which became the **Cultural Revolution** launched by Mao in 1966.

The Socialist Education Movement

Despite the damage to his reputation due to the Great Leap Forward, Mao still commanded enormous respect and authority within the Party. Liu and Deng were forced to stage a tactical retreat in the face of Mao's onslaught. The result was an uneasy compromise. Liu and Deng endorsed Mao's analysis of the situation but continued to use their own practical measures to aid economic recovery. Therefore, although rural capitalism was condemned, private plots for peasant farmers and rural markets continued to be allowed. This was not enough for Mao. The Socialist Education Movement was launched in 1964 to preach the virtues of the collective economy and the superiority of Socialism. This movement was also established to root out corruption among Party cadres, and here again the divergence between Mao's approach and that of Liu and Deng was apparent. Mao intended a nationwide mass mobilisation campaign of struggle meetings against Party officials. Under Liu's direction, the approach was much more centrally controlled and concerned with imposing discipline rather than ideological correctness. Work teams of over 10,000 cadres were sent to rural areas to investigate local leaderships and root out corruption and those guilty of economic crimes. For those on the receiving end the effect was the same whoever was in control. Thousands were executed and many more committed suicide. In Hubei province Party officials spoke of 'all hell' breaking loose in a 'violent revolutionary storm'. Mao, however, as a consistent advocate of class violence and mass struggle, was still far from happy with Liu's policies.

A growing power struggle

Until 1961 Liu Shaoqi had been seen as Mao's chosen successor. It was he who had taken over the chairmanship when Mao had stepped down at the end of 1958. In 1962, it gradually became apparent that Mao was losing confidence in Liu. Partly this was due to the critical speech Liu made at the 7,000-cadre conference. It was also due to Liu's support for the pragmatic policies adopted to aid China's economic recovery. These policies, involving a number of retreats from the collective ideals that were so vital to Mao, were taken as evidence by Mao that Liu had lost his nerve. From this came doubts that Liu could be entrusted with Mao's legacy. As his doubts grew, Mao became more outspoken in his criticisms of Liu. By late 1964 Mao was accusing Liu of 'taking the capitalist road' and being non-Marxist. He also accused Deng Xiaoping of running an independent kingdom. The battle lines were being drawn for a power struggle that would reach its climax in 1966, although neither Liu nor Deng saw themselves facing a showdown with Mao. They continued to respect him and tried to work with him, despite not agreeing to all of his policy demands.

Fig. 5 *Mao Zedong at a conference in 1962 with (left to right): Zhu De, Zhou Enlai, Chen Yun, Liu Shaoqi and Deng Xiaoping. The smiling faces of the participants hide the fact that there were growing tensions within the leadership, with Liu Shaoqi and Deng Xiaoping soon to be named as the leading 'capitalist-roaders'*

Support for Mao: the PLA

Mao built up alternative power bases with which he could bring pressure to bear on the Party leadership. One of these was the PLA under the leadership of Lin Biao, a loyal ally of Mao. Lin increased the number of Party members in the PLA and stepped up the degree of indoctrination of recruits in the army. He published a compilation of selected quotes from Mao under the title *Quotations from Chairman Mao* (otherwise known as the *Little Red Book*), which was issued to all recruits and used as the basis for political education within the PLA. With its stress on self-sacrifice, self-reliance and the importance of continuing struggle, the book was used to encourage the cult of Mao within the armed forces. In 1965, Lin Biao abolished all ranks within the PLA, which appeared to make the PLA an advanced, revolutionary, egalitarian organisation and a model for the rest of Chinese communist society. He also began to extend the PLA's influence into the internal security forces and schools, factories and cultural life. By the end of 1965 the PLA had become a highly politicised organisation, totally committed to supporting Mao and able to wield considerable influence far beyond the purely military sphere.

Support for Mao: Jiang Qing and radical intellectuals

Another source of support for Mao was a group of radical intellectuals led by Jiang Qing, his wife. In the early 1960s, Jiang rose to prominence as she spoke out, largely at Mao's behest, against writers and intellectuals who showed insufficient commitment to revolutionary values. By implication, her attacks on intellectuals were also attacks on the Party leadership for allowing 'revisionist' writings to be published. Mao had argued since the Yan'an days that art and literature should promote the revolution. During the early 1960s, however, many artists and writers had begun returning to more traditional themes in their work. For Mao and Jiang this was a dangerous trend that was made worse by the fact that Party leaders were turning a blind eye to these changes. With the central Party leadership outside his control, Mao sought support from loyal leaders in the provinces. Jiang Qing had allies among the Shanghai Party leaders who were more radical than the leadership in Beijing. Mao himself moved to Shanghai in November 1965 where he was surrounded by people very much in tune with his view that there was a pressing need to restore socialist values and discipline in the economic and cultural life of the nation.

Fig. 6 *Mao's fourth wife, Jiang Qing, when she was a young actress in Shanghai*

Cross-reference

See page 38 for more on the **Yan'an Rectification campaign**.

The **Cultural Revolution Group (CRG)** is covered in more detail on pages 98–100.

Key profile

Jiang Qing

A former Shanghai film actress, Jiang Qing (1914–91) was Mao's fourth wife. They married in Yan'an in 1939. During the 1950s, she worked for the Ministry of Culture but otherwise did not have a major political role.

The split in the leadership of the PRC created an unstable political situation that could not continue indefinitely. By the end of 1965, Mao was ready to launch his challenge to the Party leadership. He could count on the support of Lin Biao and the PLA and Jiang Qing and her radical intellectual allies in Shanghai. He could also rely on two other key allies: Chen Boda, his political secretary and a leading Party ideologist; and Kang Sheng, his security chief. Mao's challenge would come in the form of the Cultural Revolution, which he would launch in 1966.

Key profiles

Chen Boda

Chen Boda (1904–89) was a key ideological adviser to Mao. After joining the CPC in the 1920s, he went to Moscow to study and after his return became a teacher in Yan'an. During the Yan'an years he served as Mao's political secretary. During the 1950s his main role was to act as the interpreter of Mao Zedong Thought. From 1958 he also edited the Party journal, *The Red Flag*. In 1966, he became the head of the Cultural Revolution Group (CRG).

Kang Sheng

Born into a wealthy warlord's family, Kang Sheng (1898–1975) joined the CPC in the 1920s and was sent to Moscow for training in intelligence work. On his return he became the CPC's security chief in Shanghai in the early 1930s, responsible for identifying and removing Guomindang agents from the Party. During the Yan'an years he was Mao's security chief and was responsible for the purges of Party members in the 1942 Rectification campaign. During the Civil War he was in charge of land reform in Shandong and Shanxi provinces and ordered the execution of many landlords. A ruthless and effective security chief in the 1950s and 1960s, Kang lived an extravagant and corrupt lifestyle, surrounding himself with a large collection of valuable antiques confiscated from his victims.

Activity

Revision exercise

Copy and complete the following table to show the power bases for Liu and Deng and the alternative power bases being developed by Mao.

Leader	Power base
Liu/Deng	
Mao	

The personality cult of Mao Zedong

During the 1960s the CPC's propaganda department, which was dominated by supporters of Mao, deliberately created a cult of personality around him. The cult of personality had been present in the 1950s but in a much more low-key way. Using political education classes in schools, colleges, workplaces and military units, the CPC promoted *Quotations from Chairman Mao* as the source of all truth and the means to finding a solution to all problems. Mao was promoted as the Great Helmsman who had led China out of the evils of feudalism, landlordism and subservience to foreign powers into the promised land of Communism. He was the embodiment of the revolution; the revolution was Mao. By allowing this cult of personality to grow, the Party leadership were accepting a situation in which people were more loyal to Mao than they were to the Party itself.

I was thirteen in 1965. On the evening of 1 October that year, the sixteenth anniversary of the founding of the People's Republic, there was a big fireworks display on the square in the centre of Chengdu. The signals for the fireworks went off a few yards from where I stood. In an instant, the sky was a garden of spectacular shapes and colours, a sea of wave after wave of brilliance. The music and noise rose from below the imperial gate to join in the sumptuousness. After a while the sky was clear for a few seconds. Then a sudden explosion brought out a gorgeous blossom, followed by the unfurling of a long, vast, silky hanging. It stretched itself in the middle of the sky, swaying gently in the autumn breeze. In the light over the square the characters on the hanging were shining. 'Long Live Our Great Leader Chairman Mao!' Tears sprang to my eyes. ' How lucky, how incredibly lucky I am to be living in the great era of Chairman Mao Zedong!' I kept saying to myself. 'How can children in the capitalist world go on living without being near Chairman Mao, and without hope of seeing him in person?' I wanted to do something for them, to rescue them from their plight. I made a pledge to myself there and then to work harder to build a stronger China, in order to support a world revolution. I needed to work hard to be entitled to see Chairman Mao, too. That was the purpose of my life.

10   *From Jung Chang, Wild Swans, 1992*

Comrade Mao Zedong is the greatest Marxist-Leninist of our era. He has inherited, defended and developed Marxism-Leninism with genius, creatively and comprehensively and has brought it to a higher and completely new stage.

Mao Zedong's thought is the guiding principle for all work of the Party, the army and the country. Therefore, the most fundamental task in our Party's political and ideological work is at all times to hold high the red banner of Mao Zedong's thought, to arm the minds of the people with it and to persist in using it to command every field of activity.

Once Mao Zedong's thought is grasped by the broad masses, it becomes an inexhaustible source of strength and a spiritual atom bomb of infinite power.

11   *Lin Biao in the foreword to Quotations from Chairman Mao, December 1966*

■ **Exploring the detail**

Lei Feng

Lei Feng was a soldier who had died in an accident (some accounts say that he was a fiction invented by the Party). Not a hero in the conventional sense, he was held up as an example of how doing the everyday, boring things in life with a sense of duty and commitment was in itself a form of heroism. He was portrayed as an example of selflessness, the true embodiment of the revolutionary spirit of hard work and self-sacrifice. In the propaganda image of Lei Feng, he is shown as being particularly grateful to Mao for rescuing him from the evils of the past and he always read Mao's works as a way of finding solutions to problems. His adulation for Mao helped to reinforce the cult of personality and support the message that only through reading Mao's works could the Chinese reach a correct understanding of Socialism.

Activity

Source analysis

Go to **www.maopost.com** and study the following Chinese revolutionary posters by entering the reference numbers in the search box.

■ 'Chairman Mao Zedong', August 1958 (reference number 0312-001M)

■ 'Chairman Mao's great soldier, Lei Feng', October 1965 (reference number 1128-001M)

■ 'Long live Chairman Mao, our great tutor, great leader, great commander-in-chief and great helmsman', December 1966 (reference number 0958-001S)

1 Compare the 1950s poster of Mao with the one published in 1966. In what ways is his portrayal different?

2 Using all three posters, identify the key features of the cult of personality that was developed around Mao Zedong.

3 In the light of the failures of the Great Leap Forward, and from what you have learned about Chinese society at this time, how was it possible for such an uncritical view of Mao to have been accepted in China?

Learning outcomes

In this section you have looked at the beginnings of economic planning in China after 1953 and the political and economic consequences of the various Five Year Plans. Economically, the First and Third Five Year Plans achieved major progress towards the industrialisation of China, whereas the Second Plan (the Great Leap Forward) had disastrous results. There were important political consequences of the failure of the Great Leap Forward for the ruling Communist Party. After reading this section, you will have an understanding of the growing divisions within the Communist Party and Mao's attempts to reassert his authority.

AQA⁄ Examination-style questions

Study Sources A, B and C and then answer the questions that follow.

The people have taken to organising themselves along military lines, working with militancy, and leading a collective life, and this has raised the political consciousness of the 500 million peasants still further. Community dining rooms, kindergartens, nurseries, sewing groups, barber shops, public baths, happy homes for the aged, agricultural middle schools, 'red and expert' schools, are leading the peasants towards a happier collective life and fostering ideas of collectivism among the peasant masses.

In the present circumstances the establishment of people's communes is the fundamental policy to guide the peasants, to accelerate socialist construction and complete the building of socialism ahead of time.

A   *From the Central Committee, August 1958*

By May 1958 Mao had increased that year's steel target from six to eight million tons and cut the length of time needed to overtake Britain to seven years and the United States to fifteen years. Indeed, China might get there first, Mao suggested, and 'reach Communism ahead of schedule'. After that, all restraint was cast to the winds. The aim, as ever, was to make China great. 'Although we have a large population,' Mao told the Politburo, 'we have not yet demonstrated our strength. When we catch up with Britain and America they will respect us and acknowledge our existence as a nation.'

B

*Adapted from P. Short, **Mao: A Life**, 1999*

The four year leap was a monumental waste of both natural resources and human effort, unique in scale in the history of the world. Close to 38 million died of starvation and overwork in the Great Leap Forward and the famine which lasted four years. Mao knowingly starved and worked these tens of millions to death.

C

Adapted from Jung Chang and J. Halliday,
***Mao: The Unknown Story**, 2006*

(a)   Explain how far the views in Source B differ from those in Source A in relation to the motives for launching the Great Leap Forward.   *(12 marks)*

AQA
Examiner's tip   When answering part a) questions on sources, it is important to remember that both sources have to be used and referred to. The question asks 'how far', which requires you to identify both points of agreement as well as points of disagreement. It is a good idea to make a simple table with two columns for agreement and disagreement and make brief notes on each source under these headings. Note that both sources refer to the building of Socialism (or Communism) ahead of schedule. This was clearly a key motive behind the decision to launch the Great Leap Forward. There are, however, differences of emphasis between the two sources. Source A gives greater emphasis to political motives such as raising 'the political consciousness' of the peasants and 'fostering ideas of collectivism among the peasant masses'. Source B, on the other hand, focuses more on the need to make China a great power that could rival other powers such as Britain and the USA. The examiner will be looking for a balanced answer that identifies points of agreement and disagreement between the sources and then reaches a conclusion as to 'how far' the two sources differ.

(b)   Use sources A, B and C and your own knowledge.
How important was Mao's leadership in explaining the failure of the Great Leap Forward?   *(24 marks)*

AQA
Examiner's tip   This question requires you to use both the sources and your own knowledge. The omission of one or other of these elements in your answer will limit the marks you can achieve. It is important to refer to all three sources in your answer. Sources B and C are much more directly focused on Mao's leadership than Source A. The fact that Source A is a statement from the Party's Central Committee can be used to show that it was not Mao alone who launched the Great Leap Forward; you can use your own knowledge here to point out that the Central Committee, after some initial reluctance, was backing Mao's ambitious plans for the Great Leap when it issued this statement. The examiner will be looking for a balanced answer in which you identify and explain a range of factors that led to the failure of the Great Leap Forward and then finally arrive at a conclusion in which you weigh up Mao's personal responsibility against those other factors.

8 The aims, origins and course of the Cultural Revolution

In this chapter you will learn about:

- the aims and origins of the Cultural Revolution

- how the Cultural Revolution developed between 1966 and 1969.

Fig. 1 *Red Guards at a rally held in Tiananmen Square, Beijing, November 1966*

Almost a million people could fit into Tiananmen Square, and on this day [18 August] it was packed as I had never seen it before. Everywhere there was chanting, marching, and near-hysterical acclamations of 'Chairman Mao', 'Chairman Mao'. And at the centre of the rostrum stood Chairman Mao, in an olive-green PLA uniform. As he waved to the crowds, they began to cry and scream for him even harder. They think he's a god, I thought. 'We will die for Chairman Mao,' they shouted again and again.

1   *From Sirin Phathanothai, **The Dragon's Pearl**, 2006*

In 1966, Mao launched the Great Proletarian Cultural Revolution, an extraordinary and violent upheaval that threatened the very foundations of the regime he had done so much to establish. Just after 5 am on the morning of 18 August, a time carefully selected to coincide with the sunrise, Mao walked out into Tiananmen Square in Beijing to a rapturous reception from 1 million Red Guards. He wore a green PLA uniform to emphasise his warlike mood and his closeness to the army. Lin Biao, the PLA leader, addressed the crowd, describing Mao as the 'Great Leader, Great Teacher, Great Helmsman and Great Commander'. This was the first of eight such rallies in Beijing, following which the Red Guards, made up of university and high-school students, conducted a violent campaign against 'all those people in authority who are taking the capitalist road'. Parts of China descended into chaos until the movement was finally brought under control by the PLA in 1969. Although the violent phase of the Cultural Revolution ended then, its repercussions were still being felt in the 1970s and beyond.

■ The aims and origins of the Cultural Revolution

> To struggle against and overthrow those persons in authority who are taking the capitalist road, to criticise and repudiate the reactionary bourgeois academic authorities and the ideology of the bourgeoisie and all other exploiting classes, and to transform education, literature and art, and all other parts of the superstructure not in correspondence with the socialist economic base.

2   *'Sixteen Points on the Cultural Revolution' by the Central Committee, August 1966*

It was Mao who launched the Cultural Revolution and it was Mao and his allies who defined its aims and targets. However, as events unfolded the original aims of the movement were broadened and new targets were added for the Red Guards to attack. It is therefore difficult, if not impossible, to reduce the complexities of the Cultural Revolution to a single classification. For the purposes of analysis, however, it is helpful to consider the aims and origins of the Cultural Revolution under three main headings:

- a struggle to remould Chinese culture
- a power struggle within the CPC
- a rectification campaign.

A struggle to remould Chinese culture

The Cultural Revolution was an attack on all modes of thought and behaviour that did not conform to Mao's vision of a socialist society. It was to be a 'great revolution that touches people to their very souls'. By changing Chinese culture, i.e. all modes of thought and expression, and by making Mao Zedong Thought the guiding principles of the Chinese people, a truly communist society could at last be built in China. The aim was to create nothing less than a 'new socialist people'.

The first battles in the Cultural Revolution took place over a play. *Hai Rui Dismissed from Office* was written by Wu Han, an intellectual, historian and deputy mayor of Beijing. The play was about an official from the Ming dynasty (1368–1644) who was dismissed after criticising the emperor for wasting resources on extravagance while ordinary people starved. The parallels with the Peng Dehuai episode in recent Chinese history were not lost on Mao and his allies and, in November 1965, an article was published in a Shanghai newspaper attacking the play and its author. The article was written by Yao Wenyuan, one of the Shanghai 'radicals' with which Mao's wife had allied herself. In launching this attack on Wu Han the Shanghai radicals, with Mao's blessing, were also attacking the Party

■ Exploring the detail

Red Guards

The Red Guards were loose groupings of college and secondary school students who embraced the cult of Mao and the aims of the Cultural Revolution. They were formed originally to struggle against teachers in their own institutions but quickly took on a much wider role as the 'vanguard' of the revolution. Red Guards could be as young as 12 or as old as 30, but most were in their teens. They were useful allies for Mao because they were outside the official Party structures.

leadership. Wu Han's boss in Beijing was the mayor, Peng Zhen, who was also the Politburo member responsible for culture. Peng was therefore held to be responsible for allowing such 'anti-socialist' plays to be performed and, as Peng was a key ally of Liu Shaoqi and Deng Xiaoping, the Party leadership was also being attacked indirectly. The response of the Party leadership was to treat the issue as an academic rather than a political debate, and to try to keep control over events by setting up the Cultural Revolution Group to investigate the issues raised by the affair. With Peng Zhen as head of this organisation, it was clear that the Party leadership was attempting to defuse the crisis.

Key profiles

Yao Wenyuan

A radical literary critic and intellectual, Yao Wenyuan (1925–2005) began his career in Shanghai and attracted attention with his outspoken attacks on the local daily newspaper. He allied himself with radical politicians in the city. He had been prominent in the campaign against Hu Feng in the mid-1950s and had joined a group known as Proletarian Writers for Purity.

Cross-reference

See page 69 for more on **Hu Feng**.

Peng Zhen

Peng Zhen (1902–97) joined the CPC in 1923 in Shanxi province. He was imprisoned by the Nationalists in 1929 and after his release he helped to organise the communist resistance against the Japanese in north China. He became mayor of Beijing in 1951 and held the post until he was purged at the start of the Cultural Revolution in 1966.

In February 1966, the Shanghai radicals raised the stakes by issuing a statement claiming that China was 'under the dictatorship of a sinister anti-Party and anti-socialist line which is diametrically opposed to Chairman Mao's thought. This sinister line is a combination of bourgeois ideas on literature and art.' Lin Biao, the head of the PLA and a key ally of Mao, also laid down the battle lines when he stated that 'If the proletariat does not occupy the positions in literature and art, the bourgeoisie certainly will. This struggle is inevitable.' Therefore, the struggle over culture was part of the wider class struggle and, as such, could not be considered as merely an academic debate. To emphasise his support for Mao's line on culture, Lin Biao appointed Jiang Qing to coordinate the PLA's cultural policies.

Cross-reference

For more on **Jiang Qing**, see pages 92 and 124–5.

The assembly room, though cavernous, was packed. Slogans hung everywhere and Mao's *Little Red Book* bobbed in front of people's faces. When I entered, Jiang Qing was already on stage, leaping up and down as she shouted slogans in her unpleasant, high-pitched voice. 'Learn from the Red Guards' was the principal [slogan] on this occasion. 'Learn from Auntie Jiang Qing' came back the chorus. We read Mao's quotations out loud. We sang songs. We waved the *Little Red Book*.

Then she spoke. She told in minute detail how Chairman Mao had had to fight off the wicked persecution of Liu Shaoqi's revisionist *coup d'état* attempt. The audience roared its support.

3   *A meeting in the Great Hall of the People. From Sirin Phathanothai, **The Dragon's Pearl**, 2006*

As the Cultural Revolution gathered momentum, the cultural policies of Jiang Qing became clear. What Mao, Jiang Qing and their allies were attempting to do was to impose strict limits on culture to ensure that it served the revolution and that 'anti-socialist, poisonous weeds' were eradicated from the arts. In Jiang's view, art was not something to be valued for its own sake nor did it exist in a vacuum. All art reflects the society from which it springs and serves a political purpose. Therefore, a feudal society produces a feudal culture, a bourgeois society produces a bourgeois culture, etc. In a socialist society, feudal and bourgeois art forms have no place. Indeed, to allow them to be published or performed would undermine people's belief in Socialism and threaten the very foundations of the new China. It was therefore necessary, according to Jiang Qing, to completely eradicate all feudal, bourgeois and foreign influences in Chinese culture and replace them with a truly 'proletarian culture'. Mao denounced the 'Four Olds': old culture, ideas, customs and habits. Jiang Qing turned Mao's

Fig. 2 *The Four Olds*

slogan into a programme for the eradication of traditional Chinese culture. Traditional opera was suppressed and replaced by 'revolutionary operas' in which the heroes and heroines represented workers, peasants and soldiers. Literature, art, films and theatre were subjected to a strict censorship – only those works that promoted revolutionary themes were allowed. Western music was banned as being bourgeois and decadent. Wearers of Western-style clothing were liable to be attacked. Anything that was seen as representative of the past – temples, works of art, ornamental gardens – was liable to be destroyed.

The recruitment of youthful Red Guards was a key part of Mao's strategy for the Cultural Revolution. Young people would, in Mao's eyes, be untainted by the thoughts, habits and customs of old China. They could be mobilised in a campaign to eradicate the Four Olds from Chinese culture.

A power struggle within the CPC

Since the 7,000-cadre conference in 1962, Mao had been largely at odds with the Party leadership of Liu Shaoqi and Deng Xiaoping. In 1966, Mao was 73 years old. He felt that he was being denied influence over policy because of his age and he was increasingly concerned about the question of who should succeed him when he was gone. After the fall of Peng Dehuai it was Liu Shaoqi who had been promoted to the number two position in the communist hierarchy and who was therefore considered to be Mao's chosen successor. By 1965 it was Mao's view that Liu Shaoqi and his allies could not be trusted with defending and extending the revolution and Mao had decided that they should be purged. Attacking Liu and Deng directly, however, was not a wise course of action. Both had shown themselves to be loyal to Mao and the Party in the past, they had

Activity

Thinking point

1. Explain why Mao believed that it was important to wage a political struggle to change Chinese culture.

2. Why were the Four Olds and Western influences selected as targets in the Cultural Revolution?

the support of most of the Party Politburo and they enjoyed considerable prestige among the Party rank and file. Mao, therefore, acted in a devious way to undermine them and attack them at their weakest points, using the lessons he had learned many years before in guerrilla warfare.

The attack on Wu Han's play which signalled the beginning of the Cultural Revolution was, in reality, an attack on the Party leadership. Although Mao was not the author of Yao Wenyuan's article, he was undoubtedly the inspiration behind it and had sanctioned the attack. In attacking Wu Han, the article was also attacking Peng Zhen, an ally of Wu Han and the Politburo member responsible for culture. By association, the attack on Peng was also an attack on Liu Shaoqi and Deng Xiaoping. By doing nothing to stop this play from being performed, Liu and Deng had shown that they were either incompetent or they were allies of Wu Han and Peng Zhen. Either way, they were showing themselves, in the eyes of Mao and his allies, to be untrustworthy 'capitalist-roaders'.

In March 1966, while Liu was away on a foreign tour, Mao – with the support of Lin Biao, Kang Sheng and Chen Boda – made his first move against the Party leadership. Peng Zhen was removed from office by the Politburo after Deng Xiaoping and Zhou Enlai had abandoned him to his fate, calculating that to continue supporting him would threaten their own careers. Following this, in May 1966, Mao took control of the Cultural Revolution Group, which was reformed with his allies occupying the key positions. At this point Mao had seized the initiative and his objectives were beginning to become clearer, yet Liu Shaoqi and Deng Xiaoping still clung to the belief that they could both retain control over events and satisfy the Chairman's demands. Their optimism was severely tested, however, when the movement spread to the universities. In May, a large-character wall poster criticising the university administration was put up in Beijing University by a philosophy professor. This seemingly spontaneous act was, in fact, orchestrated by Mao's ally Kang Sheng, whose wife had close links with the professor. Mao endorsed the poster and ordered that its message should be broadcast on the radio, thereby spreading the movement to other campuses. By the early summer of 1966 university campuses were experiencing growing turmoil as students, armed with Mao's *Little Red Book* and wearing Red Guard armbands, began to attack their teachers and university administrators. Liu and Deng tried to contain and control this movement by sending work teams on to the campuses, whose job it was to direct the students' criticisms at specific individuals and away from the Party in

Cross-reference

Further details about **Kang Sheng** and **Chen Boda** can be found on page 92.

Exploring the detail

Large-character wall posters

Known in Chinese as *dazibao*, this form of communication had been used in China for centuries. These wall-mounted posters were hand written and used large-sized Chinese writing. They had traditionally been used as a means of protest or propaganda, or simply popular communication. In the Cultural Revolution the use of these posters by the Red Guards to denounce their victims became widespread.

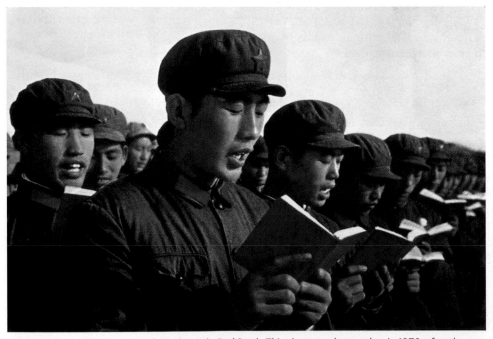

Fig. 3 *Soldiers of the PLA recite from the* Little Red Book. *This photograph was taken in 1970, after the official end of the Cultural Revolution*

general. For Mao, this was further confirmation that Liu and Deng were attempting to frustrate his wishes.

In July 1966, Mao swam in the strong currents of the Yangzi River, a symbolic act designed to show that he still had the physical strength to fight the revolutionary battles that lay ahead. With extensive newspaper and newsreel coverage, the swim in the Yangzi had enormous propaganda value for Mao. He returned to Beijing, a city he had not visited since November 1965. By staying away from the capital he had been able to distance himself

Fig. 4 *Mao [front] swims in the Yangzi River in July 1966 at Wuhan. This event, just before he launched the Cultural Revolution, was designed to show that Mao still had the energy and determination to fight*

from both the actions of the Party leadership and the early stages of the Cultural Revolution. Now he was ready to place himself squarely at the centre of events. At this point his criticism of Liu became open and direct. At a Central Committee meeting in August – the first for four years – Liu was forced to make a self-criticism for his errors in sending work teams into universities. His words were not, however, sufficient to save him. Mao accused him of exercising a dictatorship in Beijing and resisting the Cultural Revolution. The Central Committee approved changes in the CPC's hierarchy which left Liu Shaoqi demoted from second to eighth place, while Lin Biao was promoted to second place and established as Mao's chosen successor.

Deng Xiaoping had been spared from humiliation in August as Mao and his allies concentrated all their fire on Liu. At a Party conference in October, however, both Liu and Deng were subjected to more criticism and forced to make self-criticisms. Although they both officially retained their posts within the Party and the PRC, their careers were effectively over. Liu died in prison in 1969. Deng survived, largely because he enjoyed the support of Zhou Enlai, and was rehabilitated in 1973.

The purge of the Party leadership did not end with the fall of Liu and Deng. Other victims in the autumn of 1966 included Wang Renzhong (the Party chief of Hubei province), Tao Zhu, Marshal He Long and Zhu De. All these men, in the eyes of Mao, were tainted with 'old thinking' and were purged as a warning to other Party officials at all levels that they needed to show more enthusiasm for the Cultural Revolution.

Activity

Revision exercise

Make a large copy of Figure 5. Add further notes to the outer arms to give examples of how the Communists used propaganda in an attempt to control the masses.

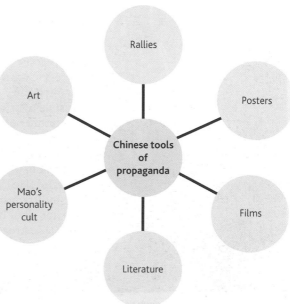

Fig. 5 *Chinese tools of propaganda*

Exploring the detail

Status in China

To be 'red by birth' in the People's Republic of China, a person had to come from a worker's, peasant's or soldier's family or be the child of a Party official. Those who did not have these connections had limited career opportunities. The Cultural Revolution gave young people from more bourgeois backgrounds the chance to prove that they were 'red by action'.

Exploring the detail

Rallies

The first enormous rally of Red Guards was held in Tiananmen Square on 18 August 1966. One million Red Guards from all over China converged on Beijing to participate in the rally at which Mao appeared. This was the first of eight such rallies held between 18 August and 26 November, involving a total of 13 million Red Guards.

Cross-reference

See page 99 for details on the Four Olds.

The extent of this outpouring of violence, and the rage of the young Red Guards against their elders, suggest the real depths of frustration that now lay at the heart of Chinese society. The youth needed little urging from Mao to rise up against their parents, teachers, Party cadres and the elderly, and to perform countless acts of calculated sadism. For years the young had been called on to lead lives of revolutionary sacrifice, sexual restraint, and absolute obedience to the State, all under the conditions of perpetual supervision. They were repressed, angry and aware of their powerlessness. They eagerly seized on the order to throw off all restraint, and the natural targets were those who seemed responsible for their cramped lives. To them Mao stood above this fray, all-wise and all-knowing.

6

*From P. Short, **Mao: A Life**, 1999*

The development of the Cultural Revolution

The starting point

The various strands in Mao's struggle to assert his dominance over the CPC had been gathering momentum since the end of 1965. On 8 August 1966, however, the Communist Party's Central Committee adopted the Cultural Revolution as official Party policy and issued a document, 'Sixteen Points on the Cultural Revolution'. This can usefully be taken as the official starting point of the 'great revolution that touches people to their very souls'. Members at this meeting also elected a new Politburo in which Lin Biao was elevated to become Vice-Chairman of the Party (and therefore Mao's chosen successor) while Liu Shaoqi was demoted. From this point onwards, events began to unfold quickly.

Mao held a series of enormous rallies in Beijing involving millions of Red Guards. In a society in which movement around the country was strictly controlled, transporting millions of Red Guards from the provinces to Beijing could only be achieved with the logistical support of the PLA. Lin Biao, the head of the PLA, was therefore a key figure in facilitating the Cultural Revolution as well as acting as Mao's chief ally and cheerleader.

By the end of August 1966, chaos and violence had spread across China. Schools and universities were closed. Red Guards were free to humiliate, beat and kill. Their targets were intellectuals, university and school teachers, members of non-communist parties and those from the 'five black categories'. The Red Guards, many of whom dressed in green PLA uniforms, also began a campaign to eradicate the Four Olds and all traces of Western influence in China. They declared war on 'Hong Kong-style haircuts, Hong Kong-style clothing, cowboy trousers, winkle pickers and high-heeled shoes'. 'Correction stations' were set up at street corners where heads of offenders were shaved. Historic sites such as temples, old city gates, statues and historical artefacts were damaged. Religious buildings in particular were singled out for attack. Red Guard units also invaded and ransacked the private homes of those suspected of being 'bourgeois'. Antiques, foreign currency, jewellery, musical instruments, paintings and books were confiscated or destroyed. Large piles of books by authors considered to be bourgeois or feudal were set on fire in city streets. Authors now considered to be bourgeois included many of the intellectuals who had participated in the May 4th Movement in 1919, a movement from which Mao and other Communists of his generation had drawn inspiration.

In the days after Mao reviewed the first group of Red Guards in Beijing, and gave them his blessing, the Red Guards in Shanghai took over the streets. The newspaper announced that the mission of the Red Guards was to rid the country of the 'Four Olds'. There was no clear definition of 'old'; it was left to the Red Guards to decide. First of all they changed street names. The main thoroughfare of Shanghai along the waterfront, the Bund, was renamed Revolution Boulevard. They smashed flower and curio shops because, they said, only the rich had the money to spend on such frivolities. The other shops were examined and goods they considered offensive or unsuitable for a socialist society they destroyed or confiscated. Because they did not think a socialist man should sit on a sofa, all sofas became taboo.

7   *From Nien Cheng, **Life and Death in Shanghai**, 1986*

Activity

Source analysis

Study Source 7. What can we learn from this source and the background information about the targets of Red Guard violence in the early stages of the Cultural Revolution?

During August and September 1966, the violence of the Red Guards continued unchecked. Many of the victims of the violence in the early stages were selected at random, but by autumn 1966 the attacks became more systematic and directed specifically at Party officials. Mao and his allies in the Cultural Revolution Group were angry that the CPC leadership had been resisting the Cultural Revolution while appearing to support it. Some officials offered up their subordinates as victims to the Red Guards in an effort to save themselves. Others encouraged the formation of Red Guard units that were more under the control of the Party bureaucracy. These so-called 'conservative mass organisations' recruited from workers and students whose parents were Party cadres. In an ironic twist, Red Guard units composed of students from bourgeois, non-Party backgrounds were the most radical and the most inclined to attack Party officials. At this early stage in the Cultural Revolution, therefore, splits and rivalries were beginning to become apparent in the Red Guards.

Fig. 7 *A poster displayed in Beijing describes how to deal with so-called 'enemies of the people', January 1967. The victim is being held in the 'jetplane' position, with head thrust forward and arms forced back*

Widening and deepening the Cultural Revolution, October 1966 to January 1967

Key events

In October 1966, at a Central Committee Work Conference, Mao, Lin Biao and the CRG stepped up their campaign against Liu Shaoqi and Deng Xiaoping, accusing them of being behind the CPC's resistance to the Cultural Revolution. Wall posters were issued denouncing Liu and Deng by name and the two leaders were forced to make a self-criticism at the conference. It was clear that Mao and the CRG were determined to intensify their assault on the CPC establishment. This marked a new stage in the radicalisation of the Cultural Revolution. For example, 20 members of the Central Committee of the Beijing district Communist

■ Activity

Thinking point

Explain why the Red Guards were becoming divided by factional rivalries in late 1966.

■ Exploring the detail

The 'January Storm'

The 'January Storm' in Shanghai actually began on 30 December 1966 with serious street battles between rival factions outside the Party offices in the city. When the rebels seized control of the city, many local government leaders were purged and Wang Hongwen became the effective leader in the city. A Shanghai people's commune was established to run the city.

Party were forced to appear before struggle meetings, at which they had to wear dunce's caps and were subjected to verbal and physical abuse.

In November 1966, militant factory and office workers began to form their own Red Guard units. In Shanghai a Workers' Revolutionary General Headquarters (WRGH) was set up, with the blessing of the CRG, to coordinate radical groups in the city. Supporters of this body were known as the 'revolutionary rebels'. The Shanghai CPC leadership tried to obstruct this new development, which was outside its control, but Mao declared that workers had the right to establish their own mass organisations and the Shanghai Party bosses were forced to make a public self-criticism. Nevertheless, the Party leadership in Shanghai supported the establishment of the Shanghai Red Detachment, a conservative mass organisation whose members, known as 'proletarian revolutionaries', opposed the efforts of the revolutionary rebels to overthrow the existing power structures. This factional rivalry quickly degenerated into violence.

At the end of December 1966 there were street battles between rival Red Guard factions in Shanghai. This was the beginning of the episode known as the 'January Storm'. Strikes paralysed the port of Shanghai and the railway network in and around the city. On 3 January 1967 the revolutionary rebels seized control of the main newspapers in Shanghai. These events brought about the collapse of the authority of the Party leadership in Shanghai. At this point, Mao intervened. He sent two loyal allies, Zhang Chunqiao and Yao Wenyuan, to Shanghai with orders to bring down the Shanghai Party Committee and establish a new political authority in its place. In the January Revolution of 5 January 1967, the WRGH announced the overthrow of the Shanghai Party Committee and declared that the city would henceforth be run by the revolutionary rebels. With the support of the PLA, the WRGH took control of all factories, docks, newspapers and businesses in Shanghai. During the rest of January 1967, rebel groups seized power in seven other provinces including Beijing.

Fig. 8 *A propaganda poster from the Cultural Revolution. Red Guards are shown denouncing an 'anti-revolutionary' book by the author Wu Han*

■ Cross-reference

Struggle meetings are covered in more detail on page 38.

See page 98 for more on **Yao Wenyuan**.

■ Key profiles

Zhang Chunqiao

Zhang Chunqiao (1917–2005) was one of the Shanghai radicals associated with Jiang Qing. With a background in propaganda, he rose to prominence during the Cultural Revolution and became deputy head of the CRG.

Wang Hongwen

Originally a textile worker from Shanghai, Wang Hongwen (1933–92) rose to prominence during the Cultural Revolution after leading the rebels in their seizure of power in January 1967. He became a close ally of Jiang Qing and the other Shanghai radicals.

In January 1967, having been arrested and interrogated, Nien Cheng was moved to a different prison in another part of Shanghai. This is her description of how the city bore the scars of several months of revolutionary upheaval.

> There was evidence of destruction everywhere; scorched buildings with blackened windows, uprooted trees and shrubs and abandoned vehicles. Debris whirled in the wind. Grey bent figures were digging hopefully among heaped rubbish. Traffic lights were not operating. Slogans covered the walls of every building we passed. They were even plastered on the sides of buses and trucks. Instead of policemen, armed soldiers patrolled the streets. We passed several truckloads of helmeted revolutionaries armed with iron rods and shouting slogans, probably on their way to carry out revolutionary actions against some rival factions.

8	
	*From Nien Cheng, **Life and Death in Shanghai**, 1986*

Activity

Source analysis

Study Source 8. What can we learn from this source about the effects of Red Guard activity on the city of Shanghai?

Mao and his allies had no plan to guide Zhang and Yao in establishing a new political authority. Having gained control of Shanghai with PLA support, Zhang established a Shanghai people's commune. This was a body whose officials would be chosen in free elections and would be subject to democratic accountability. In other words, there would be no Communist Party monopoly over elections to the commune. Following Mao's principle of 'trust the masses', Zhang believed he had Mao's support in establishing this new body. However, in a change of tack that was one of his trademarks, Mao declared that 'There must be a Party somehow. There must be a nucleus, no matter what we call it.' He refused to back the Shanghai people's commune and instructed rebel groups in other cities not to follow Shanghai's example.

In one of the key turning points of the Cultural Revolution, on 23 January 1967 the Shanghai people's commune was abandoned and replaced by the Shanghai Revolutionary Committee. This was an organisation made up of three elements – a 'three-in-one combination' in the words of Mao – consisting of 'revolutionary rebels', Communist Party officials and PLA representatives. This became a prototype for the establishment of revolutionary committees in other cities and provinces. With the Communist Party in disarray, however, it fell to the PLA to organise and support the new revolutionary committees.

The intervention of the PLA, February 1967

With the PLA taking an increasingly active role in the Cultural Revolution, the army became subject to the same stresses and strains that were dividing Chinese society. Lin Biao, the political head of the PLA, was a key driving force behind the Cultural Revolution. Many of his top military commanders, however, were determined to ensure that the PLA should be insulated from the revolutionary upheavals that were destabilising Chinese society. As the PLA had the ultimate responsibility

Fig. 9 *Propaganda work during the Cultural Revolution, showing young Chinese being given instruction on the use of weapons*

for defending the nation against external attack and for maintaining internal security, military commanders believed that the discipline and unity of the army should be maintained at all costs. This meant that PLA officers should not be subjected to struggle meetings involving criticism and humiliation, unlike their civilian political counterparts. The CRG, on the other hand, believed that no sector of Chinese society should be immune from the rectification campaign that was at the heart of the Cultural Revolution. Mao was careful not to reveal his views on this issue. He approved a directive that prohibited attacks on the PLA but did not condemn radical military cadets when they staged struggle meetings against their commanders. In the absence of clear political leadership, a number of senior military commanders decided to act on their own initiative against radical groups. In the February Crackdown, regional military commanders in Sichuan and Wuhan used armed force to suppress radical groups and arrest their leaders.

A political backlash

At the same time, the February Adverse Current developed. This was a backlash against the excesses of the Cultural Revolution by leading members of the Politburo. When, in February 1967, Mao criticised Jiang Qing and Chen Boda for taking decisions on the Cultural Revolution without consulting him, members of the Politburo who had harboured doubts about the whole concept of the Cultural Revolution began to voice their criticisms openly. They pointed out that the Red Guards had been overstepping the boundaries for the Cultural Revolution laid down in the Sixteen Points. This led to a Politburo directive, supported by Mao, which imposed limits on the use of force by the Red Guards, ordered Red Guards to stop travelling around the country and return to their native towns and cities, and directed Red Guards to withdraw from Party and government departments responsible for defence, economic planning, foreign affairs, public security, finance, banking and propaganda. The PLA was ordered to restore order.

The radicalisation of the Cultural Revolution, February to August 1967

The February Adverse Current might have been the point at which the Cultural Revolution was reined in by China's political leadership. In fact, the opposite happened. Mao saw the criticism of the Cultural Revolution from members of the Politburo as a challenge to his authority and a confirmation of his original decision to launch the attack on the Party establishment. After February 1967, the Politburo virtually ceased to function and its powers were henceforth exercised by the Cultural Revolution Group. The criticism of veteran Party cadres became bolder and more sustained. PLA officers who had attempted to crack down on radical Red Guards were denounced as ultra-rightists and court martialled. The PLA was ordered to refrain from using armed force against Red Guards. Liu Shaoqi and Deng Xiaoping, despite now being isolated and having no political influence, were also caught in the backlash against the February Adverse Current. Both were placed under house arrest.

Fig. 10 *A propaganda poster from the Cultural Revolution showing the struggle against 'revisionism'. Here, Red Guards, workers, peasants and soldiers are seen brandishing the Little Red Book and attacking a 'revisionist'*

Key events

- Factional rivalry escalated and in many places led to pitched battles between rival groups. For example, in Wuhan in July 1967, 600 people were killed in clashes between a 'conservative' workers' group called the Million Heroes and the more radical Workers' Revolutionary General Headquarters. Mao, Jiang Qing and Lin Biao sided with the radicals. The regional military commander, who had imprisoned radical leaders during the February Crackdown, was purged. Mao and Jiang Qing now began to advocate arming the radical groups in preparation for a struggle against 'capitalist-roaders in the PLA' who were supporting the more conservative mass organisations.

- There were arms seizures from transports taking Chinese weapons to North Vietnam. Regional military commanders came under renewed attack from the Red Guards.

- Radical groups in Beijing seized control of the foreign ministry and there were attacks on the British, Indian, Burmese and Indonesian legations in the capital.

The crackdown on the Red Guards, August 1967

Once again China seemed on the verge of degenerating into chaos and once again Mao underwent a major change of heart. Realising that the PLA risked being fatally undermined as a disciplined and effective fighting force, he drew back from his radical policies. On 11 August 1967 he issued a statement in which he said that the policy of 'dragging out capitalist-roaders in the army' was 'unstrategic'. This was the signal for a crackdown on radical groups and their leaders. The earlier chaos and radical excesses were conveniently blamed on the May 16 Group, a tiny radical group few people had heard about until it was named as a scapegoat. In late August, the four most radical members of the Cultural Revolution Group were purged and in September Mao approved an order that forbade Red Guards from seizing weapons. The PLA was also authorised to open fire on radical groups in self-defence.

The creation of new political structures, August 1967 to July 1968

This was another key turning point in the Cultural Revolution. After the events of August and September 1967, the main focus of the Cultural Revolution shifted from the destruction of the old order towards the creation of a new system. Mao ordered the rival Red Guards and workers' factions to unite and form 'grand alliances'. He called for rapid progress in setting up new revolutionary committees. In Beijing and Shanghai, this was achieved quickly.

Fig. 11 *Chinese leaders Zhou Enlai, Mao Zedong and Lin Biao review troops in Tiananmen Square, October 1967. Note that, in contrast to photographs from the early 1960s, Liu Shaoqi and Deng Xiaoping are no longer part of this official group, having been purged during the Cultural Revolution*

Elsewhere in China, however, factional rivalries and conflicts continued and delayed the formation of revolutionary committees. Between August 1967 and July 1968, revolutionary committees were established in 18 provinces. In the remaining provinces, which were more remote or more deeply divided, it took longer to create the new political structures.

The purging of the Red Guards, August 1967 to July 1968

Key events

- By the end of 1967 a far-reaching purge of the Red Guards was under way. Under the pretext of clamping down on the excesses of the May 16 Group, 10 million people fell under suspicion, 3 million of whom were detained for questioning. At just one of the PRC's main ministries, the foreign ministry, 2,000 officials were purged.

- In the spring of 1968, the net was widened into a campaign 'for the cleansing of class ranks', which led to the arrest of a further 1.8 million people. Tens of thousands of these victims were either beaten to death or committed suicide. Most of the rest were sent to labour camps. New public security regulations made it a counter-revolutionary crime to criticise Chairman Mao, Lin Biao or other radical leaders.

- In the summer of 1968, Mao took steps to restore order in Shaanxi and Guangxi provinces where civil war had been raging. The PLA was ordered to separate the warring factions and Military Control Commissions were established to put down resistance to military rule. In Guangxi this provoked a wave of indiscriminate slaughter, including some instances of cannibalism when so-called 'traitors' were killed and their livers eaten by their assailants.

The University itself had become a battle zone. Verbal fights had given way to pitched battles. The campus was divided into two warring states, the conservative faction and the rebel faction. Both had loudspeakers with which to blare vehement denunciations at each other twenty-four hours a day. Both pledged undying allegiance to Chairman Mao. Both were his most loyal followers, their opposites were evil incarnate. Each faction had its own armband for identification. Anyone who entered the wrong zone was sure to be pelted with stones and accused of spying. Laboratories were turned into miniature arms factories to produce tear gas and hand grenades.

9
*From Sirin Phathanothai, **The Dragon's Pearl**, 2006*

Activity

Source Analysis

Study Source 9.

1 What can we learn from this source about factional rivalries among the Red Guards in the Cultural Revolution?

2 What can we learn from this source about the effect of Red Guard activity on university education?

- There was also serious violence and disorder on a number of university campuses, including that of the large and prestigious Qinghua University in Beijing. The violence at Qinghua brought about the final suppression of the Red Guards. Arguing that the leadership of the

Cultural Revolution should be in the hands of workers not students, in July 1968 Mao sent a team of 30,000 workers and PLA troops on to the campus at Qinghua to disarm the student Red Guards. Ten people were killed in the fighting that followed.

■ The suppression of the Red Guards was followed by a large-scale, compulsory, rustication programme in which young people from the cities were sent to live and work in the countryside. Between 1968 and 1970, some 5 million young people were sent for work-study programmes among the peasants. At the same time, several million Party cadres and intellectuals were ordered out of the cities to live in May 7th Cadre Schools. For Mao, these programmes fulfilled two objectives: they forced bureaucrats to rediscover their revolutionary zeal through hard manual labour while Red Guards were forced out of the cities and dispersed to areas where they could cause little trouble.

The growing power of the PLA

The PLA played a key role in the Cultural Revolution. Not only was it responsible for restoring order, it was also assuming a much greater political role in Chinese society. Many of the rusticated youths were sent to work on army-run farms in remote border regions. PLA officers oversaw the 'cleansing of class ranks' at the May 7th Cadre Schools, while military work teams were installed in factories, newspaper offices and every government department.

The PLA was also emerging as a dominant force in the new political structures. At provincial level, half of the members of the new revolutionary committees were PLA officers; Red Guards provided one third of the members while veteran Party cadres made up only 20 per cent of these bodies. At local level, PLA dominance was even more pronounced. In some areas, 98 per cent of members of county-level revolutionary committees were drawn from the army. By the end of 1968, the last Red Guard units had been disbanded, their newspapers closed and China was effectively under military rule.

The end of the Cultural Revolution

In September 1968, when the last of the 29 provincial revolutionary committees was finally established, the Cultural Revolution Group proclaimed 'the entire country is red'. In other words, the Cultural Revolution, in the eyes of its main protagonists, had completed its work. Mao then moved to draw the Cultural Revolution to a close.

A full Central Committee meeting was held in October 1968, made up of the survivors and those who had gained from the Cultural Revolution. By the time the Central Committee met, more than two thirds of those who had been members in 1966 had been purged and only 40 members with full voting rights were present. Under the Party constitution this was not enough to make binding decisions. Acting unconstitutionally, Mao added 10 new members to the committee and packed the meeting with 80 of his supporters, drawn from the PLA and the new revolutionary committees. The Central Committee declared that the Cultural Revolution had been necessary and it had won a 'great and decisive victory'. The meeting denounced the February Adverse Current and those who had supported it but did not purge them from their posts. Liu Shaoqi, who had long since ceased to have any power but who still served as a convenient scapegoat, was finally expelled from both the Party and the government.

Exploring the detail

May 7th Cadre Schools

These were camps set up for the 're-education' of Party cadres through physical labour and political study, and through learning from the peasants. They were usually located in rural areas, far from the homes of those sent to them. Perhaps as many as 3 million people were relocated in such camps.

Activity

Preparing a presentation

'The Cultural Revolution was an act of pure destruction. Its sole purpose was to reassert Mao's position as the Red Emperor.' Divide the class into two groups. One group should prepare a presentation in support of this proposition and the other should prepare a presentation in support of Mao's declared aims during the Cultural Revolution.

This Central Committee meeting was followed by a full Party Congress in April 1969. This meeting ratified the decisions of the Central Committee and officially declared the end of the Cultural Revolution. A new Party constitution adopted by the Congress stressed the 'guiding role' of Mao's thought and the importance of continuing class struggle in the Party's ideology. The Cultural Revolution was over and Mao's position as the Red Emperor had been secured.

Meanwhile, Liu Shaoqi was ending his days as a prisoner in an unheated room at the local Party headquarters in Kaifeng. In November 1969, he developed pneumonia for a second time, but permission to move him to a hospital was refused. He died on 12 November.

Activity

Revision exercise

Copy and complete the table below. In the second column identify the main events at each stage of the Cultural Revolution. In the last column, select one event that was a key turning point in the Cultural Revolution and write a short paragraph to explain its importance.

Phase in the Cultural Revolution	Main events	Critical event
The opening shots: August to October 1966		
Widening and deepening: October 1966 to January 1967		
A critical moment: February 1967		
Radicalisation of the Cultural Revolution: February to August 1967		
The final phase: August 1967 to April 1969		

Summary questions

1 Explain why, in the early stages of the power struggle, Mao did not attack Liu and Deng directly.

2 Explain why Mao was so concerned about the Communist Party becoming bureaucratic.

3 Explain why Mao's call to arms found such an enthusiastic response among Chinese youth.

4 Explain why the Cultural Revolution was accompanied by so much violence in the years between 1966 and 1969.

9 The impact of the Cultural Revolution

In this chapter you will learn about:

- the impact of the Cultural Revolution on urban and rural areas of China

- the impact of the Cultural Revolution on education and China's youth

- the effects of the Cultural Revolution on cultural and intellectual life

- how the Communist Party was affected by the Cultural Revolution.

Fig. 1 *A propaganda poster from the Cultural Revolution, 'Chairman Mao is our heart's red sun.' A Chinese worker holds up the* Little Red Book. *In the background are people representing many other countries. Posters like this reinforced the personality cult of Chairman Mao*

Exploring the detail

Mass killings

Public spaces such as theatres, sports stadiums and town squares became the venues for systematic killings. For example, in a two-day period in the town of Daxing, 300 people were clubbed to death in the town square.

The violent phase of the Cultural Revolution lasted two and a half years. During this time there were many hundreds of thousands of deaths and many Chinese suffered beatings and imprisonment on the flimsiest of evidence, without the opportunity to defend themselves in a court of law. In the province of Guangxi alone, it has been estimated that there were 67,000 deaths in the years 1966–76. Nei Menggu (Inner Mongolia), Xizang (Tibet) and Sichuan also saw many hundreds of thousands of deaths. Extrapolations based on the figures from these provinces indicate a total death toll from the Cultural Revolution of between 700,000 and 850,000. These figures

Exploring the detail

Failure to eliminate the Four Olds

One striking example of the failure of the Cultural Revolution to eliminate old thought was in evidence in 1976 after the death of Zhou Enlai. The Festival of the Dead ceremony in Tiananmen Square, a ritual that had its origins in the Confucian idea of reverence for ancestors, was attended by tens of thousands of people.

Cross-reference

For more on the **Festival of the Dead ceremony,** see page 134.

Activity

Thinking point

'The Cultural Revolution was in many ways a device for Jiang Qing to pursue her personal agenda.' Explain why you agree or disagree with this view.

Fig. 7 *A propaganda poster from the Cultural Revolution showing the leading role played by Jiang Qing*

The campaign against the Four Olds, and the incitement of youthful Red Guards to rebel, had one lasting effect. The attack on Confucian principles meant that it became a counter-revolutionary crime to show respect for the aged or one's parents. Old thought and old customs were never completely eradicated, however, nor did Mao and Jiang Qing succeed in their aim of remoulding the people – their habits, customs, ideas, attitudes, loyalties and motivations. Changing people proved to be much more difficult than changing institutions or systems.

Exploring the detail

Kang Sheng's execution squads

Kang Sheng, a close ally of Mao and the head of the Central Case Examination Group (a form of political police force), was given a free hand to use violence and torture. In Yunnan province, 14,000 Party cadres were executed at the hands of Kang Sheng's 'police'. In Nei Menggu (Inner Mongolia), 350,000 were arrested, of whom 89,000 were beaten and maimed and another 16,000 killed. There were also large numbers of executions in Hebei, Guangdong and Shanghai.

Cross-reference

Further details about **Kang Sheng** can be found on page 92.

The impact on the Communist Party

Since 1949 the CPC had been the cornerstone of the political power structure in the People's Republic of China. As the 'vanguard' party, the CPC was involved in, and had control over, political decision-making and the implementation of policy at all levels. In theory, the CPC was organised on the basis of the Leninist theory of 'democratic centralism'. In other words, Party members at the lower levels in the organisation had the right to be involved in discussions about Party policies, but it was the collective leadership of the Party through the Central Committee, the Politburo and the Party Congress that made the final decisions. Once decisions had been made by the Central Committee, and ratified by the Party Congress, Party members at the lower levels were expected to accept and implement these policies. Party members had the theoretical right to appeal to higher authority if they wished to take issue with the way policies were being implemented, but in practice the exercise of this right would lay the members open to charges of factionalism, right-oppositionism and counter-revolutionary crime. Lower-level Party cadres were, therefore, under pressure to conform and accept unquestioningly the policies handed down from above. Successive purges during the 1950s and early 1960s had reinforced the authoritarian tendencies within the Party leadership and strengthened Mao's position.

The Cultural Revolution was conceived by Mao partly as another purge of the CPC. This time the purge cut a deep swathe through all ranks of the CPC. Higher ranking officials were affected most. Over 70 per cent of provincial and regional officials, including four out of six Regional Party First Secretaries, were purged. At national level, over 60 per cent of higher-ranking officials lost their jobs; only 9 of the 23 Politburo members of 1966 survived the purge. At local level, about 20 per cent of the Party bureaucracy were labelled as 'revisionists' or as 'persons in authority taking the capitalist road'; 3 million cadres were sent to May 7th Cadre Schools where they were forced to undertake hard physical labour and intense ideological study. Most of these people survived the Cultural Revolution and were later rehabilitated but a large number were tortured, beaten to death, died of exhaustion and malnutrition, or committed suicide.

With so many experienced Party cadres falling victim to the Cultural Revolution, it is perhaps surprising that the CPC survived at all. It seemed in the early months of the Cultural Revolution, when officials were being hounded out of office by the Red Guards who were heeding Mao's call to 'Bombard the Headquarters', that Mao's aim was to replace the CPC with some other form of revolutionary organisation. A critical point in the power struggle was reached in January 1967 when revolutionary activists began to seize power from the Party bureaucracy in Shanghai and moved to establish a people's commune in which the CPC would no longer have a vanguard role. Mao was forced to make a choice. Should he allow this new revolutionary organisation to replace his Party or would he draw back and defend the CPC's vanguard role? His answer was unequivocal: 'You can call it what you please, Communist Party or Socialist Party, but we must have a Party. This must not be forgotten.'

During 1967 and 1968 Mao's focus began to shift away from the destruction of the old order towards the creation of a new one. Alongside the drive to establish revolutionary committees in which the CPC exercised a leadership role, Mao also set about rebuilding and restructuring the CPC. Arrangements were put in place for the election of a new Central Committee and the convening of a national Party Congress. Recruitment of new members was resumed and many former Red Guards were absorbed into the CPC, although only if they could demonstrate that they came from the correct 'worker-peasant-soldier' class background.

Fig. 8 *'The Red Army victorious', a propaganda poster from the 1950s*

Activity

Challenge your thinking

Mao had been committed to the Communist Party for the whole of his adult life. How far did he destroy the old CPC during the Cultural Revolution?

A new Party constitution was drawn up. The meetings of the new Central Committee in October 1968 and of the Party Congress in April 1969 set the seal on these changes in the Communist Party. The composition of the delegates to the Party Congress, however, reflected the profound changes that the CPC had undergone as a result of the Cultural Revolution. Of the 1,500 delegates to the Congress, two-thirds were members of the PLA. The PLA also dominated the new Central Committee, with 45 per cent of the membership. The ranks of the veteran cadres of the CPC had been decimated by the Cultural Revolution. The new members of the Party, even at the level of the Central Committee, were less well educated, less experienced and more likely to be slavish adherents of Mao Zedong Thought than the veteran cadres they had replaced. With Mao Zedong Thought enshrined as the guiding principles of the CPC, and a new Party constitution that was more open to manipulation than the one it replaced, Mao now had an even more compliant party than the one that had existed before the Cultural Revolution.

Mao's purge of the Party had succeeded. Liu Shaoqi, Deng Xiaoping and several other leading members of the Politburo had been humiliated, removed from office and neutralised as a political force. Indeed, the Politburo itself had ceased to have any real power; its place had been taken by the smaller Standing Committee that consisted of Mao, Lin Biao, Zhou Enlai, Chen Boda and Kang Sheng. The question of the succession to Mao had been clearly settled in favour of Lin Biao. However, these outer appearances were deceptive. Although the PLA's position had been strengthened, Lin Biao's position was by no means secure. The struggle for the succession to Mao was set to continue. With weakened political institutions and a fragmented political leadership, China was about to experience a period of political instability that would last beyond Mao's death.

Activity

Revision exercise

Copy and complete the table below. Using the information in this chapter, list groups or individuals under each of these headings.

Victims of the Cultural Revolution	Beneficiaries of the Cultural Revolution	Survivors of the Cultural Revolution

Summary questions

1. How far was the Chinese education system damaged by the Cultural Revolution?

2. "The Cultural Revolution had little effect on the peasants". Explain why you agree or disagree with this view.

3. How successful was the Cultural Revolution in achieving Mao's aims for social change in China?

10

The aftermath of the Cultural Revolution

In this chapter you will learn about:

- the power groupings and factional rivalries after the Cultural Revolution

- the reasons for and the impact of the fall of Lin Biao in 1971

- the anti-Confucius campaign and the rise of the Gang of Four

- the rise of Deng Xiaoping and his developing struggle with the Gang of Four over the succession to Mao.

Fig. 1 *Chairman Mao greets former US president Richard Nixon on a visit to Beijing in February 1976. Nixon had previously visited China in 1971 when he was still president*

In 1969, Mao was 76 years old. The Cultural Revolution, which he had launched, had been hailed a 'great and decisive victory'. The Ninth Party Congress had officially declared that the Cultural Revolution was over. As a struggle for power, however, the Cultural Revolution was far from over. Indeed, a new and more turbulent phase was about to begin, made all the more bitter and urgent because Mao was nearing the end of his life and the question of the succession was in everyone's minds. Moreover, the Cultural Revolution continued to define political debate in China. Until Mao's death in 1976, the key criterion on which any policy was judged was whether or not it conformed to the 'verdict of the Cultural Revolution'. Factional rivalry within the Communist Party reflected a key divide within political ranks: 'survivors' of the Cultural Revolution tended to be on the more moderate, pragmatic wing of the Party whereas 'beneficiaries' of the Cultural Revolution tended to favour radical policies.

Power groupings and factional rivalries after the Cultural Revolution

In the aftermath of the Cultural Revolution, there were three main power groupings within the Chinese political system:

- Lin Biao and the PLA
- Jiang Qing and the Shanghai radicals
- Zhou Enlai and the bureaucracy.

■ Exploring the detail

Relations with the USSR

Relations between the USSR and China had been deteriorating since the late 1950s but in 1969 there were violent clashes between the armies of the two powers. The Soviet Union had been building up its forces on China's western frontier in Xinjiang province and on the northern frontier of Manchuria. Mao feared that this was the precursor to a full-scale attack on China. In March 1969, he decided to pre-empt the Soviets by provoking a clash over a disputed island in the Ussuri River, on the northern frontier. The most serious battle cost up to 100 Soviet lives and about 800 Chinese killed. There were several more clashes between the two armies over the spring and summer of 1969 before a peace settlement was agreed in September.

■ Activity

Thinking point

Mao had always believed that 'the Party controls the gun'. Why then was he becoming concerned about the PLA's position in Chinese political life after the Cultural Revolution?

Lin Biao and the PLA

The PLA had been accorded a special status in the PRC since its victory in the Civil War. The army was held up by Mao as an exemplar of revolutionary discipline and virtue. 'The whole country should learn from the PLA' was one of Mao's quotations which was frequently used in banners and posters. The crucial role played by the PLA during the Cultural Revolution, particularly during the latter stages when it was used to restore order and clamp down on Red Guard excesses, gave the PLA an enhanced prestige and a higher profile in the political life of China. We have seen in Chapter 9 how the CPC's Central Committee meeting in October 1968 and the Ninth Party Congress in April 1969 were dominated by PLA representatives. The new revolutionary committees at regional, provincial and local levels were also dominated by the PLA. Events in 1969 further raised the prestige of the army. Armed clashes with Soviet troops on the border between China and the USSR created a sense of national crisis and placed the PLA once again in the role of defenders of the nation.

Attempts by Mao after 1969 to rebuild the CPC as an essentially civilian political party made slow progress at first. Despite efforts to recruit new members and establish new Party branches and Party committees, the PLA continued to dominate the Party at local and provincial levels. It had always been a guiding principle of Maoism that the Party should control the military. In the aftermath of the Cultural Revolution, there was the potential for these roles to be reversed. Signs of Mao's concerns about the potential dangers of this situation can be detected in his tendency to add these words to his earlier quotation: 'The PLA should learn from the people of the whole nation.'

As Commander-in-Chief of the PLA, Defence Minister in the government of the PRC and a member of the Party Politburo's Standing Committee – and as Mao's nominated successor – Lin Biao exercised enormous power. Throughout the Cultural Revolution Lin Biao had been one of the key figures in promoting the cult of Chairman Mao. He wrote the introduction to the *Little Red Book*. In his speech to the Ninth Party Congress, Lin had taken the lead in praising the 'genius' of Chairman Mao: 'Chairman Mao always charts the course. In our work we do no more than follow in his wake.' Lin had won Mao's trust by being passive and compliant; in the wake of the triumphant Ninth Party Congress, however, he began to show himself to be more confident and self-important.

Jiang Qing and the Shanghai radicals

Jiang Qing, Mao's fourth wife, had risen to prominence in Chinese political life through the Cultural Revolution. As she was close to Mao, she was a useful ally to those who wished to gain his trust and advance their own political careers. Therefore, although she was (in the words of a recent biographer of Mao, Philip Short) 'shallow, vindictive and totally self-centred', she was able to

Fig. 2 *Mao Zedong with Lin Biao. After the purge of Liu Shaoqi, Lin was named as Mao's successor and played a leading role in the Cultural Revolution*

make powerful alliances and extend her own influence. She had been closely associated since 1965 with a group of Shanghai radicals which included Zhang Chunqiao, Yao Wenyuan and Wang Hongwen. Through the Shanghai Forum on literature and art in the armed forces, held in February 1966, she had forged a close alliance with Lin Biao. She had also established close links with Mao's security chief, Kang Sheng. Through the Cultural Revolution Group these powerful figures had been, together with Mao himself, the driving forces behind the Cultural Revolution and had developed an alliance with the more radical Red Guard units. The Red Guards provided Jiang and her allies with their mass base and enabled them to pursue their radical political and cultural agenda. By 1969, Jiang Qing, Zhang Chunqiao and Yao Wenyuan were elevated to the CPC's Politburo, a recognition of their enhanced status as a result of the Cultural Revolution.

The official end of the Cultural Revolution, however, appeared to bring a reduction in the power and influence of Jiang and her Shanghai radical allies. The Red Guards had been disarmed by the PLA and millions of former Red Guards were forced to leave the cities. The Cultural Revolution Group was wound up in 1969 and Mao appeared to be swinging away from the 'ultra-left' policies that Jiang and her group had promoted. On the other hand, in November 1970 Mao gave this group control over the Central Committee's Organisation and Propaganda Group, through which they could exercise enormous power over Party affairs, propaganda and the media.

The relationship between Jiang Qing and Lin Biao had become increasingly strained since they forged their alliance in 1966. Because they shared broadly the same policy objectives, the differences between them were mainly a power struggle. Each sought to outmanoeuvre the other in a contest to win Mao's favour. Since Mao habitually played factions off against each other, there was ample scope for this power struggle to develop. As well as being increasingly at odds with Lin Biao, Jiang Qing was unremitting in her efforts to undermine Zhou Enlai, the State Premier.

Activity

Thinking point

Jiang Qing was one of the key beneficiaries of the Cultural Revolution. How strong was her position in Chinese political life by 1970?

Zhou Enlai and the bureaucracy

As State Premier (Prime Minister), Zhou Enlai was in charge of an enormous State bureaucracy. His priorities were political stability and continuing economic growth. Zhou's great strengths were in quiet, cautious, behind-the-scenes negotiation and diplomacy. In other words, he was a pragmatist, skilled in the art of compromise. Such qualities did not sit well with the radical, ultra-left agenda pursued by Mao, Jiang Qing and their allies since the early 1960s. In communist Chinese politics, however, Zhou was the great survivor. He survived by adapting and being able to read Mao's coded signals, and then putting forward suggestions that Mao supported but did not feel able to put forward himself. He also survived by knowing when to withdraw support from former allies and colleagues when it was clear that their fate had already been sealed.

Such a pragmatic approach was in complete contrast to that of Jiang Qing. Whereas for Zhou the key test of a policy was whether it would work, Jiang Qing and her allies stressed the need for ideological purity and revolutionary zeal. Both believed that they had, or could, win the support of Mao in their struggle. In the early 1970s, education and the economy became the key battlegrounds in the factional rivalry between these two groupings.

Activity

Revision exercise

Copy and complete the table below to show the three main power groupings in China after the Cultural Revolution.

Power grouping	Support base	Ideology

The fall of Lin Biao

Fig. 3 *Mao Zedong and Zhou Enlai meet a representative of the workers at the Ninth Party Congress*

In 1969, Lin Biao appeared to be the man who had gained the most from the Cultural Revolution. Nevertheless, within months of the Ninth Party Congress, where he had been officially named as Mao's successor, Mao was beginning to have doubts about Lin's ambitions and reliability. No one had done more than Mao to undermine the CPC and bolster the position of the PLA and Lin Biao, its Commander-in-Chief. However, in a change of tack that was so characteristic of Mao, he began to criticise the PLA for 'carelessness' and 'arrogance' in the way it had carried out the purge of Party cadres. He also expressed concern about the way Chinese society seemed to be under military control. From his study of Marx's writings, Mao had learned to be wary of over-powerful military commanders who might attempt to use their power to establish a military dictatorship; in Mao's eyes Lin Biao was beginning to appear as a potential **Chinese Bonaparte**.

Relations between Mao and Lin Biao started to deteriorate in March 1970 when the Party's Central Committee met to consider proposals for a new State constitution. Mao wanted to abolish the post of State Chairman (Head of State or President), which had been vacant since the fall of Liu Shaoqi. In typical Mao fashion, however, he refrained from personally proposing or categorically endorsing this proposal. Lin Biao, however, made strenuous efforts to persuade Mao to keep the post. This immediately caused Mao to be suspicious. It was uncharacteristic of Lin Biao, who was normally passive and compliant towards him, to question his decisions. Mao suspected that Lin

Key term

Chinese Bonaparte: As students of Marx, the Chinese communists were aware of the dangers that a revolution could lead to a military dictatorship. Marx had pointed to this danger as one of the key lessons of the French Revolution of 1789–99. Napoleon Bonaparte, a military leader who owed his rise to the revolution, had deposed the government of the new French Republic in 1799 and established a military dictatorship.

harboured ambitions to become State Chairman himself, a move that would raise his status within the CPC hierarchy and possibly leave Mao sidelined into a more ceremonial role. He was also angered by the fact that Lin had enlisted the support of Chen Boda, his longstanding and trusted ideological adviser. When Chen launched an attack on Zhang Chunqiao, an ally of Mao's wife, for opposing Lin Biao, Mao denounced this as factionalism. Chen was arrested and forced to make a self-criticism. With his strong power base in the PLA, however, Lin appeared still to be in a strong position. Events over the coming months were to show just how fragile that power base was.

By the end of 1970 Mao had decided to move against Lin Biao. During 1970–1, in a series of moves he described as 'throwing stones, mixing in sand and digging up the cornerstone', Mao gradually whittled away at his power base. 'Throwing stones' meant forcing Lin's allies to make self-criticisms. 'Mixing in sand' meant undermining Lin's control of the Military Affairs Commission by adding Mao loyalists to this body. Finally, 'digging up the cornerstone' meant reorganising the key Beijing military region. Mao needed to be sure that the troops in the capital would be loyal to him rather than Lin in the event of a confrontation between them. Allies of Lin among the military commanders in Beijing were transferred to other areas.

> Today he uses sweet words and honeyed talk to those whom he entices, and tomorrow puts them to death for fabricated crimes. Looking back at the history of the past few decades, do you see anyone whom he had supported initially who has not finally been handed a death sentence? His former secretaries have either committed suicide or been arrested. His few close comrades-in-arms or trusted aides have also been sent to prison by him.

1   *Lin Biao's thoughts on Mao, probably written by his son*

By February 1971 it was clear to Lin that his position was becoming untenable. Unlike other Chinese communist leaders who had fallen foul of Mao but quietly accepted their fates, Lin decided to fight back. His son Lin Liguo, with Lin Biao's support, began preparing plans for a possible coup. Although the option of a peaceful seizure of power was not ruled out, the conspirators laid plans for the possible assassination of Zhang Chunqiao and Mao himself. When Mao undertook a tour of the provinces in August and September 1971 to enlist the support of provincial Party and PLA officials, Lin realised that the clash was coming to a head and instructed his son to activate the plans for a coup. Mao, who may have been aware of Lin's plans, took careful precautions to conceal his whereabouts and called in senior military commanders for crisis talks. At this point Lin and his son decided to fall back on their alternative plan to flee to the south in an air force jet and set up a rival regime in Guangdong. Word of their plans, however, reached Zhou Enlai. He attempted to prevent the plane from taking off but was unable to do so, although his intervention did stop the aircraft from being fully refuelled. Lin and his son were able to take off but decided to head for the USSR rather than southern China. With insufficient fuel to reach its destination, the aircraft crashed in Outer Mongolia, killing all eight people on board. Following his death, Lin was denounced as a 'renegade and a traitor' who had been working as a Soviet agent.

Activity
Source analysis
Study Source 1.
1. What can we learn from this source about Lin Biao's attitude towards Mao?
2. Compare this source with Source 11 on page 93. What possible factors might explain this change in Lin Biao's attitude towards Mao?

Exploring the detail
A coup?
This whole affair surrounding Lin Biao is shrouded in doubts and uncertainties about whether he actually planned a coup. One version is that Lin's son was the main person involved and Lin himself had little knowledge of the plan. Lin's daughter also played a key part in the way the events unfolded. She was convinced that her father was being manipulated and had been kidnapped by her brother, so she alerted the security guards to their plans to flee. It was her actions that led to Zhou Enlai's intervention, which prevented the plane from being fully refuelled.

Activity
Thinking point
1. Why did Lin Biao fall out of favour with Mao so soon after the Cultural Revolution?
2. Summarise the impact of the fall of Lin Biao on:
   a Mao Zedong
   b ordinary Chinese people.

The impact of the fall of Lin Biao

Mao had survived this attempted coup but the episode had a major effect on the Chairman and the political situation in China:

Fig. 4 *The fall of Lin Biao*

■ Senior military commanders who had been allies of Lin Biao in the Politburo were purged. His son's allies, including junior air force officers, were also purged. Despite this, the PLA retained a powerful presence within the Party and the government.

■ Mao's health was seriously affected by Lin's betrayal. Emotionally and physically shattered, he was bed-ridden for the next two months and never fully recovered his health.

■ Mao's reputation undoubtedly suffered from the revelations that the Chairman's chosen successor had been plotting his assassination. It brought into question Mao's judgement and revealed to the wider public that the higher echelons of the CPC were riddled with intrigue.

■ For many Chinese, the Lin Biao affair was a turning point in their unquestioning loyalty to Mao. It undermined their faith in both the system and Mao himself. The image of Mao as 'infallible' had been shattered. After 1971, in the assessment of Mao's biographer Philip Short, 'general cynicism prevailed'.

Activity

Revision exercise

Make a rough copy of Figure 4. Writing next to the steps, chart the main reasons behind the fall of Lin Biao.

When Liu Shaoqi was dragged down we'd been very supportive. At that time Mao was raised very high; he was the red sun and whatnot. But the Lin Biao affair provided us with a major lesson. We came to see that the leaders up there could say today that something is round; tomorrow that it's flat. We lost faith in the system.

| 2 | *An urban youth living in a village at the time* |

■ The anti-Confucius campaign and the rise of the Gang of Four

Fig. 5 *The Gang of Four. From left to right: Zhang Chunqiao, Wang Hongwen, Yao Wenyuan and Jiang Qing. These photographs were taken in 1975 and 1976, before their fall from power*

The fall of Lin Biao reopened the question of the succession to Mao. There were, in Mao's eyes, no obvious candidates to fill the gap left by Lin Biao's treachery. For Mao, this was a vital question as he was looking for someone he could trust to ensure that his ideological legacy would continue after his death. In other words, the chosen successor would have to be someone closely identified with the aims of the Cultural Revolution. Among the top CPC leadership in 1971 there were no obvious candidates. Zhou Enlai was too old and too moderate. Mao's wife, Jiang Qing, was loyal and ideologically pure but widely detested. She has been described by Mao's biographer, Philip Short, as 'greedy for power, haughty, vain and incompetent'. Although she was married to Mao, he was becoming increasingly irritated by her and saw less and less of her. In 1974, he told the Politburo that Jiang Qing 'does not represent me, she only represents herself'. Jiang Qing's ally, Zhang Chunqiao, had also risen to prominence as a result of the Cultural Revolution and had displayed some leadership qualities, but he was too closely associated with the radical faction and did not have the stature to command respect across the whole Party. No one else among the Politburo leaders had the leadership qualities that would be required to lead the CPC after Mao's death. Without a clearly designated successor, factional rivalry was bound to increase. In 1971, Mao was still a commanding presence within the CPC. As his health deteriorated, however, he became less able to dominate and the factional rivalry within the CPC leadership, which Mao himself had helped to create, became more open, more bitter and more damaging.

In 1972, in the immediate aftermath of Lin Biao's fall, it appeared that Zhou Enlai and the moderates were very much viewed in a positive light. The CPC's official response to the Lin Biao affair accused him of being a 'sham Marxist political swindler' who had 'cunningly incited ultra-left trends of thought'. Since the charge of ultra-leftism could equally well be applied to Jiang Qing and her allies, this was a coded criticism of their ideological line. Zhou used his position to restore order and discipline in industry, thereby stimulating production. He also began to argue the case for increased contact with Western capitalist powers in order to acquire advanced technologies and employ foreign experts. This was part of his broader strategy of the **Four Modernisations** to achieve higher rates of economic growth and greater prosperity. As part of this strategy, Zhou was involved in the decision to invite the American president, Richard Nixon, to China in 1972 for talks on reopening diplomatic and trade relations between the two countries. In the wake of the Nixon visit there was some relaxation of cultural policy to allow Western orchestras to visit China. Zhou also set about rebuilding the education system after the Cultural Revolution. In 1973, examinations were reintroduced as criteria for university entrance.

Despite his success in promoting a more pragmatic approach to policy-making, Zhou was unable to remove the radicals from their positions of influence. Indeed, it was the radical Zhang Chunqiao rather than Zhou Enlai who was chosen to host the farewell banquet for President Nixon, a clear sign that the radicals still had Mao's backing. Further signs of Mao swinging his weight behind the radicals came in 1973, when he announced that Lin Biao's betrayal had not happened because he was an ultra-leftist; in fact, declared Mao, Lin had been a revisionist who had adopted 'a Left appearance to disguise [his] Right essence'. In other words, this exonerated the radicals and, by implication, Mao himself from any blame in the Lin Biao affair. By the time of the CPC's Tenth Party Congress in August 1973, the radicals had recaptured the ideological high ground and appeared to be consolidating their position within the

Exploring the detail

'Ping-pong diplomacy'

In 1971, the USA table tennis team, while playing in a tournament in Japan, was invited to visit China to play some matches there. When they arrived they were the first official visitors from the USA to be received in China since 1949. The invitation was approved at the highest level of the Chinese leadership and was the first signal that the Chinese communist government wanted to re-establish contacts with Western powers. Following the success of 'ping-pong diplomacy', President Nixon visited China in 1972 and other Western leaders followed suit in later years.

Exploring the detail

Nixon's visit to China

Richard Nixon (US president 1969–74) visited China in February 1972. This was an event that shocked the world in view of the deep hostility that had existed between China and the USA since 1949. The USA still backed the nationalist regime in Taiwan and was heavily involved in the Vietnam War. However, with worsening relations between China and the USSR, Mao took the view that 'My enemy's enemy is my friend.' Trade between China and the USA improved after the visit but full diplomatic relations between the two countries did not begin until 1979.

Key term

Four Modernisations: the four modernisations were the development of agriculture, industry, national defence and science and technology.

Thinking point

Mao had, at different times, nominated Liu Shaoqi, Lin Biao and Wang Hongwen to be his successor.

1 Why was Mao so concerned about choosing who should succeed him after his death?

2 What problems had he encountered with the first two of his chosen successors?

3 Why was he having great difficulty in finding a suitable candidate in the early 1970s?

■ Exploring the detail

Confucius and Mao

Confucius had lived in the 5th century BC and his philosophical teachings had retained their influence down the centuries. To Communists such as Mao, Confucianism represented the corrupt, reactionary past.

Party hierarchy. Of the nine appointed to the key Politburo Standing Committee, three were associated with the radicals whereas Zhou Enlai had only one ally. The radicals also controlled the media and propaganda, including the most influential Chinese newspaper, the *People's Daily*.

At the Tenth Party Congress Mao unveiled his new choice for the succession. Wang Hongwen had risen to prominence in Shanghai during the Cultural Revolution and had been closely associated with the radical faction in that city. He came from a poor peasant family, had fought in the Korean War and had recently been working in a textile mill in Shanghai. Therefore, he combined all the key elements of the 'correct' class background – worker, peasant and soldier – that Mao considered essential in a true Communist. During the Cultural Revolution Wang had proved his Maoist ideological credentials by giving his wholehearted support to its aims. In 1973, Mao promoted Wang to the position of Vice-Chairman of the Party with a seat on the Politburo Standing Committee and a position of number three in the hierarchy behind Mao and Zhou. This was Mao's device for presenting Wang to the Party as his chosen successor.

At the same Congress Mao also agreed to the rehabilitation of Deng Xiaoping who, along with Liu Shaoqi, had been a major target of the Cultural Revolutionaries' assault on 'capitalist-roaders' and 'revisionists'. Unlike Liu, Deng had survived the Cultural Revolution. He had long experience in government and, with Zhou Enlai suffering from a terminal illness, Mao brought Deng back into the fold as an understudy to Zhou. It was also Mao's intention that Deng should work alongside Wang Hongwen; Deng would keep the administration functioning while Wang would assume control of the Party. This way there would be a balance of experience with inexperience, veteran cadres with younger leaders and moderates with radicals. Such a balance, in the context of post-Cultural Revolution China and with Mao's health deteriorating rapidly, was inherently unstable. Indeed, almost as soon as the Tenth Party Congress was over, Jiang Qing and the radicals launched a determined assault to undermine and remove Zhou Enlai and the moderates.

In 1973, Jiang Qing launched the anti-Confucius campaign. The campaign, which received extensive coverage in the media and dominated political activities for the next two years, was presented as a struggle between those who wanted to go forward with Communism and those who wanted to turn back the tide of history. The real target of this campaign, of course, was not Confucius. Lin Biao was now being described as 'one of the Confuciuses of contemporary China'. The attack on Confucius was also an attack on Lin Biao and his followers, but even Lin Biao was not the main target. This was Zhou Enlai. Zhou's pragmatic policies on the economy, education and contact with foreign powers appeared, in the eyes of the radicals, to threaten the ideological legacy of the Cultural Revolution. Zhou now came under attack from Jiang Qing for treason and for 'being too impatient to wait to replace Chairman Mao'. An attack on Zhou was also an attack on Deng Xiaoping because the two worked closely together.

■ A closer look

Zhang Tieshen

The radicals' attack on Zhou was fought on a number of fronts. The increased cultural contacts with the West after Nixon's visit were attacked for undermining Chairman Mao's revolutionary line in art and literature. The reintroduction of examinations for university entrance was an affront to the Cultural Revolutionary approach whereby admission should be based on the class background and ideological purity of the candidate. To highlight the revolutionary purity of their policy, the radicals publicised the case of Zhang Tieshen, a young man who had been sent to work in the countryside for five years and had therefore been deprived of formal schooling. At his university entrance examination Zhang handed in a blank sheet of paper, with a note saying that he had been too busy working 18 hours a day to study. Zhang's case was taken up by the radicals who argued that he should be admitted to university on the grounds of his revolutionary commitment alone.

The economy was another battlefront. In opposition to the pragmatic policies of Zhou and Deng, the radicals pushed for the expansion of communes, the removal of incentive payments and private plots and for an end to 'technology transfer' from the West. 'Learn from Dazhai' became a slogan that summarised the radicals' approach to economic policy. Dazhai was a production brigade in Shanxi province that had achieved increased agricultural and industrial production through applying the Maoist principles of mass mobilisation, self-reliance and incessant hard work. Dazhai was held up as an example of how communes could achieve the Maoist goals of 'narrowing the differences between town and country, workers and peasants, manual and mental labour'.

■ A closer look

'Learn from Dazhai'

The slogan 'Learn from Dazhai' had been coined by Mao in 1964 during his battles with the 'capitalist-roaders'. Dazhai was a production brigade of 83 families, part of a larger commune of about 12,000 people. It was situated in a remote, hilly, dry and barren area of Shanxi province, where the peasants had long been poor and prone to disasters. Dazhai was upheld as a model of what could be achieved by applying Maoist virtues of hard work, self-reliance and collective labour. Hillsides had been terraced, fields irrigated and farming mechanised and the harvests had produced outstanding results. Peasants were allowed no private plots and incentive payments were not allowed, which gave substance to Mao's vision of an egalitarian, socialist society. Throughout the Cultural Revolution and after, the Dazhai brigade was the model commune where visitors from China and overseas were taken. After Mao's death, however, it was revealed that the production figures from Dazhai had been consistently falsified and the commune had been heavily subsidised by payments from the State. It had all been a propaganda exercise to prove that Mao's approach was correct.

Mao undoubtedly supported the radicals' campaign, at least in its initial stages. For him the priority was to combat any signs of revisionism and protect the Cultural Revolution's achievements. As had often happened in the past, however, Mao miscalculated. The campaign went further and took on a direction he had not intended. Under the orders of Jiang Qing and her radical allies, the anti-Confucius campaign became another battlefront in the factional war against Zhou Enlai and Deng

■ Exploring the detail

Technology transfer

Despite the success of China's nuclear weapons and space programmes, the Chinese economy generally was lagging behind the West by the early 1970s. Zhou Enlai championed the policy of 'technology transfer' by which China would purchase foreign equipment and in some cases whole industrial plants from Western capitalist countries. China would also employ foreign experts to help in the modernisation of its industries, particularly the energy and aerospace industries. Under this programme the Nippon Steel Corporation of Japan built a complete steel plant at Wuhan in 1974. Rolls Royce of Great Britain signed a $100 million agreement in 1975 to build jet engines in China.

Activity

Revision exercise

Create a simple timeline to show the development of the power struggle between the Gang of Four and the moderates (Zhou Enlai/ Deng Xiaoping) from 1972 to 1975. At each point on the timeline, try to show which group appeared to have the upper hand.

Exploring the detail

The events in Tiananmen Square

The events in Tiananmen Square were watched by the Communist Party leadership through binoculars from the safety of the Great Hall of the People. The divisions within the leadership were clearly demonstrated when Zhang Chunqiao put down his binoculars, turned to Deng Xiaoping and accused him of having organised the demonstration. He denounced Deng as an 'ugly traitor'.

emphasis on improving living standards and ignoring class struggle. Deng was accused of wanting to 'reverse the verdict' of the Cultural Revolution. During October and November 1975 Mao, despite his growing infirmity, made clear his opposition to the policies being pursued by Deng. Deng retained his positions within the Party, State and army hierarchies but the withdrawal of Mao's support effectively deprived him of power.

The death of Zhou Enlai in January 1976 ushered in a new phase in the factional power struggle. Zhou had been the most popular of the revolutionary leaders after Mao himself. One million people lined the route of his funeral procession in Beijing. Using their control of the media, the Gang of Four ensured that newspaper reports of the public outpouring of grief at Zhou's death were suppressed. In March 1976, a Shanghai newspaper, on the instructions of Zhang Chunqiao, published an article that implied that Zhou had been a 'capitalist-roader'. This sparked a spontaneous reaction of support and sympathy for Zhou. Starting with student protests in Nanjing, the movement spread to Beijing when the Nanjing students' slogans, which had been painted on the sides of railway carriages, appeared in the capital. In early April, at a Festival of the Dead ceremony held in Tiananmen Square to honour Zhou Enlai, over 2 million people attended to lay wreaths and pay their respects. The event quickly turned into a political protest when posters began to appear carrying attacks on Jiang Qing (the 'mad empress'), her allies (the 'wolves and jackals') and Mao himself (the 'Qin Emperor'). At the end of the day the police were ordered to remove all wreaths and posters from the square, but the following day 100,000 people demonstrated there demanding that the tributes to Zhou be replaced. After a day in which demonstrators clashed with the police, several arrests were made and the demonstrators were dispersed with the aid of the army. Many, possibly hundreds, were summarily executed for taking part in this protest. Such spontaneous demonstrations were without precedent in communist China, a society in which any public demonstration previously had been organised by the Party. The events of Tiananmen Square in April 1976 were a sign that Mao and the Party were beginning to lose control of events.

Fig. 8 *Mourners stand together in grief as they wait to see the body of Zhou Enlai, January 1976*

You must be mad
To want to be an empress!
Here's a mirror to look at yourself
And see what you really are.
You've got together a little gang
To stir up trouble all the time,
Hoodwinking the people, capering about.
But your days are numbered …
Whoever dares oppose our Premier
Is like a mad dog, barking at the sun –
Wake up to reality.

| **4** | *A poster displayed in Tiananmen Square,*
with a poem attacking Jiang Qing |

Activity

Source analysis

Study Sources 4 and 5. What can we learn from these sources about the attitude of ordinary Chinese citizens towards the two sides in the power struggle?

This mass display of sentiment for Zhou Enlai very quickly developed into a mass movement of resentment against the radicals, including Mao himself. No name was mentioned, but veiled comparisons of him were made to the First Qin Emperor [259–210 BC], generally regarded as a cruel ruler who had persecuted scholars and destroyed books, setting back China's cultural development. The wording of the poems became less ambiguous and the sarcasm against Jiang Qing and her associates became bolder. To go to Tiananmen Square became a must for the young people of Beijing.

| **5** | *From Nien Cheng, **Life and Death in Shanghai**, 1986* |

A meeting of the Politburo, from which Deng was absent, condemned these events as 'a counter-revolutionary incident' and held Deng responsible. Mao was informed and signalled his agreement with this verdict. Two days later Deng was dismissed from all his posts, although he was allowed to keep his Party membership. Realising the seriousness of his situation, he had already left Beijing and, with the support of the local military commander, gone into hiding in Guangzhou. The fall from grace of Deng Xiaoping gave Mao the impetus to make his final choice of successor. This was to be Hua Guofeng. Already appointed as Premier to replace Zhou Enlai, Hua was now promoted by Mao to be first Vice-Chairman of the Party.

Key profile

Hua Guofeng

Hua Guofeng (born 1921) came from a younger generation of communist leaders who had been a beneficiary of the Cultural Revolution. He took part in the Long March and joined the CPC's anti-Japanese resistance in 1938. He became CPC first secretary in Henan after the Cultural Revolution before being promoted to the Politburo in 1973. Known as a capable administrator, he was also neutral in terms of the factional rivalry of the 1970s.

With Deng in disgrace, the Gang of Four were in a much stronger position to dominate the political agenda. In May 1976, Mao suffered the first of a series of heart attacks and his health rapidly deteriorated thereafter. He was no longer capable of giving any clear

把反击右倾翻案风的斗争进行到底

Fig. 9 *A propaganda poster from 1976 criticising 'Right Deviationism'. This reflects the last propaganda campaign initiated by the Gang of Four, who were increasingly unpopular in China*

leadership and the factional rivalry intensified. The radicals regarded Hua Guofeng as a political upstart and believed that they could outmanoeuvre him just as they had brought down Deng Xiaoping. During the summer of 1976 they worked hard to undermine Hua. This was a serious tactical mistake as it drove Hua to seek alliances elsewhere, particularly with the PLA military commanders. When the Gang of Four placed the 100,000-strong Shanghai militia on the alert in August 1976, this was a clear sign that they were preparing for an armed confrontation. Whatever their personal political preferences, the PLA military commanders perceived their primary responsibility as the maintenance of order and stability and the avoidance of Civil War.

As Mao approached death, the factional struggle over the succession was reaching its peak. The Gang of Four controlled the media and considered their position to be very strong. Their victory over Hua, however, was by no means guaranteed.

Summary questions

1. By 1976, the Gang of Four gained the upper hand in the power struggle to control the succession.' Explain why you agree or disagree with this view.

2. "Mao made a miscalculation in the anti-Confucius campaign." Explain why you agree or disagree with this view.

3. How important was the legacy of the Cultural Revolution to political life in China in the early 1970s?

11 Mao's death and his impact on China

In this chapter you will learn about:

- the positive achievements of Mao's rule over China

- the costs of Mao's regime for the Chinese people.

The East is Red

The east is red, the sun is rising
China has brought forth a Mao Zedong
He amasses fortune for the people
Hurrah, he is the people's great saviour.

Chairman Mao loves the people
He is our guide
To build a new China
Hurrah, he leads us forward!

This song, *The East is Red*, became the unofficial anthem of the People's Republic of China during the Cultural Revolution. Schoolchildren started the day by singing this song, as did many adults at their place of work. Loudspeakers broadcast it on the streets of China's cities. It is a stark illustration of the personality cult that surrounded Mao from the mid-1960s until his death in 1976.

Fig. 1 *Mao Zedong lies in state, September 1976*

Mao died on 9 September 1976. Hua immediately succeeded to all the top positions within the Party, State and military hierarchies and made his preparations for a showdown with the Gang of Four. They then committed another serious tactical error. Obsessed though they were with endlessly quoting Mao Zedong Thought, they ignored one of the basic Maoist principles of guerrilla warfare – when faced with a superior enemy force, withdraw to a secure base area. Their secure base area was in Shanghai, yet they remained in Beijing after Mao's death – at the heart of the government system controlled by Hua Guofeng. On 6 October 1976, with the support of the PLA, Hua arrested the Gang of Four. The factional rivalry that had bedevilled China since the Cultural Revolution was over. There would be no civil war. Deng Xiaoping was rehabilitated (for the second time) in 1978 and would succeed Hua as Chairman and supreme leader in 1980. Despite all his efforts to ensure that his legacy was entrusted to someone who would defend the 'verdict' of the Cultural Revolution, Mao had been unable to prevent the old 'number two capitalist-roader', Deng Xiaoping, from returning to power.

Activity

Source analysis

Study Sources 1 and 2.

1 What can we learn from these sources about the attitude of the CPC leadership towards Mao after his death?

2 How far do you agree with Chen Yun's assessment of Mao's life?

Had Mao died in 1956, his achievements would have been immortal. Had he died in 1966, he would still have been a great man. But he died in 1976. Alas, what can one say?

1   *From Chen Yun, 1979*

His merits are primary, his errors secondary, in the proportion of seven to three.

2   *An official Chinese verdict on Mao's life, 1981*

Since Mao's death in 1976 the Communist Party has continued to rule China. However, the China of the early 21st century is very different in many ways from the China that Mao ruled over. Since 1981, under the leadership of Deng Xiaoping and his successors, the country has experienced unprecedented economic growth and become one of the world's leading economic powers. Much of this has been achieved by abandoning many of Mao's most distinctive policies, such as rural communes, and by allowing the development of private enterprise. Although many of Mao's policies have been cast aside, the communist leadership in China has not abandoned the myth of Mao because to do so would undermine the foundations on which their rule is based. Mao's achievements have been the subject of debate and re-evaluation since his death, but he is still honoured as the founder of the PRC and his body is preserved in a mausoleum on Tiananmen Square.

Mao's achievements

Mao had many talents and qualities that equipped him for his role as leader of China. He possessed great charisma and was highly intelligent. He was a visionary, a philosopher, a poet and a highly gifted political and military strategist. However, there were also limitations to his attributes as a leader. He was no administrator – he had no enthusiasm for the mundane, day-to-day business of government. He had only a limited understanding of economics and little or no grasp of foreign affairs. Mao was first and foremost a revolutionary leader who believed in the necessity for constant class struggle and in the mobilisation of the masses.

Revolution has more to do with tearing down the old than with painstakingly constructing the new. Mao's legacy was to clear the way for less visionary, more practical men to build the shining future that he could never achieve.

3

*From P. Short, **Mao: A Life**, 1999*

When assessing Mao's achievements, therefore, we must bear in mind that Mao did not concern himself with the details of economic reform or improvements in health and education. These were essentially the work of able administrators and political leaders at all levels in the communist system of government. Mao's contribution was to 'clear the way' and set the course.

Under Mao's leadership, China was transformed in a number of ways:

- After many years of weakness and disunity, China became once again a united country. Warlordism and civil war was ended and a strong central government was established in Beijing.
- China became a great power. For more than a century foreign powers, especially Western powers and Japan, had treated China as virtually a colonial territory. Under communist rule, China regained its independence, pride and self-respect. China acquired nuclear weapons and entered the space race.
- There was progress towards greater equality for women.
- China's population became better educated and more healthy.
- Food production, particularly grain, kept pace with the rapid increase in population; apart from the period of the Great Leap Forward, hunger and starvation were largely eradicated.
- Improved communications enabled food to be moved from regions where there was a surplus to regions where there were shortages.
- China experienced significant industrial development. Steel production tripled between the 1950s and the 1970s. The foundations were laid for China's own oil industry. A machine-tool industry and

Fig. 2 *Mao's achievements*

Activity

Revision exercise

Summarise Mao's achievements under the following headings: Political; Military; Economic development; Social change.

a nuclear industry were created from scratch. Electricity generation, particularly hydroelectric power, was greatly expanded.

■ The net output of industry grew at an annual average of 10.2 per cent between 1957 and 1979. This compares favourably with the international average for other low-income countries of 5.4 per cent over the same period.

■ The costs of Mao's rule

Mao, who for decades held absolute power over the lives of one quarter of the world's population, was responsible for well over seventy million deaths in peacetime, more than any other 20th century ruler.

> **4**   *From Jung Chang and J. Halliday, **Mao: The Unknown Story**, 2006*

Official Chinese reports and estimates by historians give different figures for the numbers of Chinese who died from purges, land reform, famine and events such as the Cultural Revolution. Whatever the true scale of the deaths, it is clear that tens of millions of Chinese suffered violent deaths at the hands of the communist authorities (or at the hands of people incited to use violence as an instrument of State policy) and many millions more died from the famine of the early 1960s. In Mao's defence it might be argued that he rarely gave personal instructions for the executions carried out in his name. It could also be argued that the famine victims were the unintended casualties of his misguided policies. However, Mao showed a callous indifference to the suffering of millions of his fellow countrymen, regarding their deaths as unavoidable and as a necessary cost to bear in the pursuit of his ideals. For him, the end justified the means.

Activity

Talking point

'The deaths of millions of Chinese were a necessary consequence of the drive to modernise and strengthen China.' Organise a class debate on this issue, and consider whether you feel that the end justified the means.

There was also in Mao's China a complete indifference to the concept of human rights and the rule of law. The Chinese state exercised its power in an arbitrary way and the victims of Mao's policies had no right of appeal or protection in law. Those arrested for 'counter-revolutionary crimes' could find themselves subjected to oppressive interrogation, imprisonment without charge or trial and years spent in forced labour camps enduring physical abuse by their guards, back-breaking labour and inadequate food. Many failed to survive this treatment. Freedom of speech, conscience, assembly and protest were irrelevant in a State that showed no respect for such 'bourgeois' abstractions.

As a revolutionary Mao brought fundamental change to China but he failed to follow through on his achievements in many areas. By the 1970s China had reached an economic 'plateau'; the foundations for industrial growth and improved food production had been laid, but Mao's policies of mass mobilisation, struggle and self-reliance could not take China any further in its economic development. Economic growth was slowing down. This was the conundrum that lay at the heart of the debate between radicals and pragmatists in the 1970s. The stress on self-reliance and China's increased isolation during the Cultural Revolution had denied China access to the more advanced technologies of the West. Attacks on intellectuals and the disruption to China's education system had discouraged innovation and experiment, leaving the country unable to develop its own advanced technologies. Centralised planning of the economy had led to wasteful duplication of effort. Agriculture had benefited from irrigation schemes and other land improvements but farming was starved of both the investment needed for greater mechanisation and the use of fertilisers. The result of all this was that the incomes of ordinary Chinese peasants and workers rose very slowly, but incomes of city dwellers rose faster than the incomes of the peasants. Mao's aim of reducing inequality in Chinese society, particularly the gap between the urban population and the peasants, was as far from realisation in 1976 as it had been in the 1950s. No wonder the peasants continued to complain about 'socialism which we cannot eat'. Whereas in the 1950s Mao had been leading China towards a solution for its chronic economic under-development, by the 1970s he had become part of the problem, an obstacle to further progress.

Throughout his time as an absolute ruler, Mao had been used to getting his own way. When, as in the early 1960s, he felt he was being sidelined, he was ruthless in his determination to overthrow those leaders whom he believed were following the 'capitalist road'. He believed that by carefully selecting his successor and struggling against those who deviated from his line, he could ensure that his ideas would survive his death. Ultimately he failed in this. The vast majority of Chinese, traumatised by the Cultural Revolution, had grown tired of mass campaigns and disorder. He had dominated the years 1949–76 in China but he was unable to dominate after his death.

Activity

Thinking point

Who benefited the most from Mao's policies under the communist regime: city dwellers or peasants?

Activity

Thinking point

Draw up a balance sheet of Mao's rule, showing the positive achievements alongside the failures and costs of his policies.

Fig. 3 *PLA soldiers read copies of the* Little Red Book

Learning outcomes

This section has covered the Cultural Revolution and its aftermath between 1966 and 1976. After reading this section, you should have gained an understanding of the reasons why Mao launched the Cultural Revolution in 1966, how the Cultural Revolution developed into a violent upheaval in the years 1966–9, and how this violent phase was brought to an end. You should also have an understanding of how the Cultural Revolution had a profound impact on the lives of ordinary Chinese people and the ruling Communist Party. The impact of the Cultural Revolution on China's political life was still being felt in the 1970s as a bitter power struggle developed to control the succession to Mao. This chapter has provided a brief outline of the positive and negative aspects of Mao's rule. After reading this chapter, and by referring back to earlier chapters in this book, you should be able to evaluate the impact that Chairman Mao made on China.

AQA Examination-style questions

Study Sources A, B and C and then answer the questions that follow.

On May 15 I had to attend a final briefing. The leaders of the Workers' and Soldiers' Mao Zedong Thought Propaganda Team once again praised the first group going down [to the countryside] and then solemnly declared, 'The cadres going down are sent by Chairman Mao among the poor and lower-middle peasants to learn from them. You will be most enthusiastically welcomed by commune leaders and the peasants as their own. When you arrive at your village tomorrow, the peasants will have everything ready for you. A clean house for you to live in, rice and wheat flour for you to eat, a vat of clean water for you to drink, and farm tools for you to work with. Long live the victory of the proletarian revolutionary line of our Great Leader, Chairman Mao.

A   *Adapted from Wu Ningkun, **A Single Tear**, 1993*

In the evening of 21 December 1968 Chinese radio reported a decree from Chairman Mao: 'It is essential that school-leavers go to rural areas to be re-educated by poor and lower-middle peasants.' Shortly after the broadcast, various orchestrated activities took place. Since the start of the Cultural Revolution, each time Mao issued a new order the routine was for the streets of Beijing to be packed with hundreds of thousands of residents, mobilised for propaganda performances. Marching towards Tiananmen Square, the crowds carried red flags or huge banners urging 'Respond with Resolution to Chairman Mao's call.'

Chairman Mao was showing his public support for a new national scheme launched several months previously, which aimed to send middle-school pupils to the countryside, as more than ten million were stuck in schools. Although none had completed the courses cut short by the Cultural Revolution, they were now regarded as graduates, ready to leave. There was no prospect of further education, since universities had stopped teaching, and little chance of employment. We were told that participation would be voluntary, but at the same time it was made clear that for school-leavers in the cities, the only choice was to be re-educated by peasants in rural settlements where we were expected to spend the rest of our lives.

B   *Adapted from Aiping Mu, **Vermilion Gate**, 2000*

An immense number of youthful Chinese had been sent to the countryside – allegedly to boost production there but also to ease overcrowding in the cities – during the Cultural Revolution. Over sixteen million urban youths were resettled in these years, one million of them from Shanghai. This vast programme of relocation might have eased some social problems caused by crime and overcrowding in the big cities, but it also led to terrible personal disturbance and hardship for those unused to rural labour. Few of those ordered to live out their lives in impoverished rural areas can have shared the cheery official estimate that these young people were 'growing healthily in the vast and resourceful rural areas'.

C   *Adapted from J. D. Spence, **The Search for Modern China**, 1990*

(a) Explain how far the views in Source B differ from those in Source A in relation to the process of sending students to the countryside during the Cultural Revolution. *(12 marks)*

When answering part a) questions, remember that the question asks 'how far' the views of one source differ from those of the other. It is important to identify points of agreement and disagreement. Both sources are taken from personal reminiscences of the period but are written by two people whose personal circumstances were not exactly the same. Neither source gives any information about what actually happened to the students when they arrived in the countryside; the focus of both sources is on the process of selecting and sending the students there. The main areas to concentrate on in your answer are the role played by propaganda and encouragement of the students, placed alongside the role played by compulsion. As always, the examiner will be looking for clear and precise references to the sources, a balanced answer that identifies points of agreement and disagreement and a clear conclusion in which you come to a judgement on how far the sources differ.

(b) Use sources A, B and C and your own knowledge. How successful was the programme of 're-education through labour' in solving the social problems caused by the Cultural Revolution? *(24 marks)*

When answering part b) questions, note that the question requires you to use both the sources and your own knowledge. Failure to refer to one or the other would mean that you cannot gain the higher marks. Remember that your references to the sources should be clearly indicated. It is important to use and refer to all three sources. The question requires knowledge of the social problems caused by the Cultural Revolution and you should set out these problems at an early stage in the essay. You could, for example, refer to the lack of educational and employment opportunities for young people. It would be useful to explain what Mao was trying to achieve through the 're-education through labour' programme – in other words, his belief that time spent among the peasants would strengthen the revolutionary spirit of young people from the cities. It is important that you keep your answer focused on the question throughout, that you cover a range of social problems and that you bring your answer to a clear and balanced conclusion.

5   Conclusion

In this book you have studied a relatively short period in China's history – just 30 years in the history of a country that can trace the origins of its civilisation back through several millennia. It would not be an exaggeration, however, to argue that those 30 years were of vital importance in laying the foundations for the emergence of China as one of the most powerful nations in the world in the 21st century.

The revolution of 1911 had swept away the old, inefficient and weak imperial rule and set China on a course towards modernisation. However, it had left China internally divided and externally vulnerable to the imperialist ambitions of Western powers and Japan. The revolution of 1911 had also not led to the creation of a stable system of government that commanded the widespread support of the Chinese people.

The victory of the Communists in the Civil War led to the unification of China under a stable form of government. This government did not have the democratic consent of the majority of the Chinese people but it did, at least, have their acceptance. The success of the many mass mobilisation campaigns in the 1950s may be quoted as evidence that the communist regime was able to draw on the Chinese people's positive desire for change.

Central to the Communists' aims of making China a self-reliant, independent and proud nation once again was the need to develop the economy. Agricultural productivity had to be increased if China was to be able to feed its rapidly growing population without relying on imports and the development of heavy industry was essential if China was to achieve prosperity for its people and become a great power. The drive for economic growth, however, revealed tensions and conflicts inside the communist regime. For Mao, the priority was always to maintain ideological purity. He emphasised the need for continuing class struggle to protect the revolution from its enemies, both internal and external; his goals were equality, collective rather than individual effort, self-sacrifice and self-reliance. Other leading Communists, most notably Liu Shaoqi and Deng Xiaoping, believed that the priority should be economic growth, even if that involved compromising some deeply held convictions by allowing peasants to have their own private plots and receive incentive payments, thereby allowing some to become more successful than others. These tensions reached their climax in the Cultural Revolution.

Mao succeeded in eradicating the 'capitalist-roaders' through the Cultural Revolution, but he failed to ensure that whoever succeeded him would continue his legacy. The Cultural Revolution did little more than guarantee that a power struggle would develop within China in the last years of his life and in this struggle even Mao's personal support was not sufficient to guarantee his chosen successor a smooth transition to power. Mao had led the Communist Party to the position where it monopolised political power in China. This situation has continued since Mao's death, but the Communist Party that rules China in the 21st century is pursuing very different policies from those for which Mao had fought.

Appendix 1

Note on the transcription of Chinese words into English

Two main systems have been used to transcribe Chinese into English. Most books published before the 1980s used the older Wade-Giles system. Using this method, China's capital city was known as Peking and the subject of this book was known as Mao Tse-tung. This book uses the Pinyin system of transcription which is now in common usage. Therefore, Beijing is the name of the Chinese capital and Mao Zedong is the name of the subject of this book. The names of people, cities and provinces in China are all given in their Pinyin form, except for Chiang Kai-shek and Sun Yat-sen. Both of these names are given in the older, but more familiar, Wade-Giles styles rather than the less well-known Pinyin versions, Jiang Jieshi and Sun Zhongshan.

For the most part, pronunciation of consonants in the Pinyin style are much as they would be in English, but there are some exceptions. Thus *c* is pronounced *ts*, *q* is pronounced *ch* and *x* is pronounced *sh*. There are many variations with vowel sounds. So Deng (as in Deng Xiaoping) is pronounced *dung*; *chen* rhymes with *men*; *ei* (as in Beijing) rhymes with *say*; *ao* (as in Mao) rhymes with *cow*; *ou* (as in Zhou) rhymes with *toe*. There are too many variations to be covered adequately in this book. For a more detailed guide to Chinese pronunciation, see Philip Short, *Mao: A Life*, 1999 pages xii to xiii.

Table 1 is a select list of Chinese names that appear in this book, with both the Pinyin and the Wade-Giles versions.

Table 1 *Some Chinese names*

Pinyin	Wade-Giles
Beijing	Peking
Guangzhou	Canton
Guomindang	Kuomintang
Jiang Jieshi	Chiang Kai-shek
Jiang Qing	Chiang Ching-kuo
Mao Zedong	Mao Tse-tung
Shanxi	Shansi
Sichuan	Szechuan
Sun Zhongshan	Sun Yat-sen
Yan'an	Yenan
Yangzi River	Yangtze River
Zhou Enlai	Chou En-lai

Appendix 2

Provinces and autonomous regions (ARs) of China

Province or AR	Location	Capital city	Notable geographic features
Anhui	East central	Hefei	Fertile plain in north, mountainous in south; Yangzi River flows through mountains
Fujian	South-east	Fuzhou	Coastal region; mostly mountainous with sub-tropical climate
Gansu	North central	Lanzhou	Mostly barren desert; mountainous; large Hui ethnic minority
Guangdong	South-east	Guangzhou	Coastal, fertile land; China's richest province; sub-tropical climate
Guangxi AR	South	Nanning	Mountainous, with southern coastline; sub-tropical climate; home of Zhuang ethnic minority
Guizhou	South-west	Guiyang	Mountainous; sub-tropical climate
Hebei	North-east	Shijiazhuang	Mountainous in north and west; rest of province is part of vast North China Plain
Heilongjiang	North-east	Harbin	Much wilderness; very hard winters
Henan	East central	Zhengzhou	Fertile plain of Yellow River
Hubei	Central	Wuhan	Middle stage of Yangzi River, which flows through the Three Gorges dam; eastern and central Hubei are fertile plain with a sub-tropical climate
Hunan	Central	Changsha	On middle reaches of Yangzi River; mountains occupy 80% of province; sub-tropical climate
Jiangsu	East	Nanjing	Coastal; lower reaches of Yangzi River
Jiangxi	South-east	Nanchang	Mountainous with sub-tropical climate
Jilin	North-east	Changchun	Mountainous in south of province; very cold winters
Liaoning	North-east	Shenyang	Centre of heavy industry; central area is flat, the rest is mountainous; monsoon climate
Nei Menggu AR (Inner Mongolia)	North	Hohhot	Desert and grassland; home of Mongol ethnic minority
Ningxia AR	North	Yinchuan	Largely dry, semi-desert region, with Yellow River flowing through; home of Hui ethnic minority
Qinghai	West central	Xi'ning	Mountains and desert on Tibetan plateau; large Tibetan ethnic minority population
Shaanxi	North central	Xi'an	Dry plain of Yellow River; desert in north; mountainous in south
Shandong	East	Jinan	Mountainous (name means 'mountains east') although much of the province is part of North China Plain; on the lower reaches of the Yellow River; temperate climate
Shanxi	North central	Taiyuan	Mountainous (name means 'mountains west'); mostly dry
Sichuan	West central	Chengdu	Mountains and rivers; sub-tropical climate in south and east
Xinjiang AR	North-west	Urumqi	Deserts; rich in minerals; home of Ughur ethnic minority
Xizang AR (Tibet)	West	Lhasa	High plateau (name means 'the roof of the world'); home of Tibetan people
Yunnan	South-west	Kunming	Mostly high plateau
Zhejiang	East	Hangzhou	Coastal plain; more hilly inland; sub-tropical climate

Glossary

A

Agricultural Producers' Cooperatives (APCs): a stage towards the collectivisation of agriculture. Peasant families retained ownership of their land but shared labour, tools and equipment on a permanent basis. Their incomes came from sharing the profits of the cooperative based on the amount of land they owned.

C

cadres: officials working within the CPC and State administration.

Central Committee: an elected body that theoretically had the power to make decisions over policy in the CPC.

commandist: a term used by Mao to describe the way Party officials used their power to command (direct) the people rather than consult with and listen to them.

communes: a basic level of local government in the countryside. The people's communes of the Great Leap Forward were a radical experiment in communal living and were held up as the models for a future socialist society.

Confucianism: this was the official ideology in China before 1911 and was used to legitimise the rule of the different dynasties.

D

danwei: meaning 'work unit', the basic unit of economic, social and political life in urban China. Workers lived in the *danwei*, which also provided schools, health care and social security for the elderly. It was the focal point of political organisation in the cities.

G

Gang of Four: the group of radical Maoists who helped Mao to launch the Cultural Revolution

and were among the main beneficiaries from it. Jiang Qing, Wang Hongwen, Zhang Chunqiao and Yao Wenyuan engaged in a bitter power struggle with Liu Shaoqi and Deng Xiaoping to secure the succession after Mao's death, but they were arrested, tried and jailed by Hua Guofeng.

L

Little Red Book: compiled by Lin Biao in the early 1960s, this book is a collection of extracts from Mao's writings and speeches. It became the Maoist radicals' key text during the Cultural Revolution.

M

May 4th Movement: also known as the New Culture Movement, it took its name from a demonstration on 4 May 1919 against the high-handed behaviour of the Western allies in giving former German territories in China to Japan. This was a catalyst for many young Chinese to engage in political activity and explore Western ideas of democracy, anarchism and Marxism.

May 7th Cadre Schools: labour camps established during the Cultural Revolution, where inmates combined hard physical labour with political re-education through the intensive study of Mao's writings.

mutual-aid teams: the first stage in the move towards cooperation in agriculture, introduced in the early 1950s. Individual peasant families owned the land but were encouraged to share (temporarily) their tools, equipment and labour.

N

Northern Expedition: a military campaign undertaken by allied Guomindang and communist forces (the National Revolutionary

Army) in 1926–8 to end the rule of the warlords and unify China under one government.

P

People's Liberation Army (PLA): formed in 1946 from the various communist forces that had fought against the Japanese, the PLA evolved into a formidable, professional army during the 1950s. All units of the armed forces in China, including the navy and air force, came under the PLA.

Politburo: a shorthand term for political bureau, this body was elected by the Central Committee to be the Party's main decision-making body. In practice, decisions were taken by the smaller Standing Committee of the Politburo.

proletariat: a term used by Marx to describe the poorest class in society – those without any property. In Chinese terms, the proletariat comprised industrial workers, soldiers, peasants and State employees.

Q

Qing dynasty: the dynasty that ruled China from 1644 to 1911. The Qing originally came from Manchuria.

R

rectification: the name given to a number of campaigns by Mao to ensure the dominant role of his ideology within the CPC. The first campaign took place in Yan'an in 1942.

renminbi: the official currency in China (the people's currency). Also known as the yuan.

U

United Front: the policy of cooperation between the CPC and the Guomindang. There were two periods of cooperation: a) 1923–7, when the two combined against the warlords until Chiang Kai-shek turned his forces against the Communists in Shanghai; b) 1937–45, when there was an unstable alliance against the Japanese.

W

warlords: these were powerful provincial leaders who established their own armies and created local power bases after the collapse of the Qing dynasty. They effectively ruled their territories as independent kingdoms and even after the Northern Expedition the warlords remained key power-brokers in the Guomindang state.

Y

Yangzi River: the longest river in Asia (5,520 km; 3,430 miles), flowing from Qinghai eastwards to enter the sea at Shanghai. Usually regarded as the dividing line between north and south China, the mouth of the river is a large, fertile delta region that is one of the most prosperous and highly populated areas in China.

Yellow River: the second longest river in China (4,660 km; 2,900 miles) flowing from Qinghai northwards through Nei Menggu (Inner Mongolia) then south and east to enter the sea in Shandong province. It is a river that frequently floods, causing devastation and loss of life.

Bibliography

Students

Breslin, S. (1998) *Mao: Profiles in Power*, Longman.

Jung Chang and Halliday, J. (2006) *Mao: The Unknown Story*, Vintage.

Lynch, M. (1998) *The People's Republic of China Since 1949*, Hodder and Stoughton.

Short, P. (1999) *Mao: A Life*, John Murray.

Stewart, G. (2006) *China, 1900–1976*, Heinemann.

Teachers and extension

Gittings, J. (2006) *The Changing Face of China*, Oxford.

Macfarquhar, R. (ed.) (1993) *The Politics of China*, Cambridge.

Feuerwerker, A. and Fairbank, J. (1987) *The Cambridge History of China*, Cambridge.

Spence, J. D. (1990) *The Search for Modern China*, Norton.

Personal reminiscences

Aiping Mu (2000) *Vermilion Gate*, Abacus.

Gao Yuan (1987) *Born Red*, Stanford.

Jung Chang (1992) *Wild Swans*, Flamingo.

Nien Cheng (1986) *Life and Death in Shanghai*, Grafton.

Sirin Phathanothai (2006) *The Dragon's Pearl*, Simon and Schuster.

Wu Ningkun (1993) *A Single Tear*, Hodder and Stoughton.

Wu, H. and Wakeman, C. (1994) *Bitter Winds*, John Wiley.

Zhang Xianliang (1992) *Grass Soup*, Secker and Warburg.

Zhisui Li (1996) *The Private Life of Chairman Mao*, Chatto and Windus.

Acknowledgements

The author and publisher would like to thank the following for permission to reproduce material:

Extracts from *Wild Swans* reprinted by permission of HarperCollins Publishers Ltd. © Jung Chang (1991).

Source Texts:

p23 Adapted from a report by an American consul in Shenyang, May 1947, quoted in J. D. Spence, *The Search for Modern China*, Norton, 1990; p138 An official Chinese verdict on Mao's life, 1981 quoted in P. Short, *Mao: A Life*, Murray, 2004; p85 J. Becker, *Hungry Ghosts*, John Murray, 1996; p94 The Central Committee, August 1958 quoted in P. Short, *Mao: A Life*, Murray, 2004; p97 The Central Committee, *Sixteen Points on the Cultural Revolution*, August 1966, quoted in P. Short, *Mao: A Life*, Murray, 2004; pp25, 47, 51, 54, 73, 84, 93, 118 Jung Chang, *Wild Swans*, Flamingo, 1992; pp47, 64, 85, 95, 117, 119, 140 Jung Chang and J. Halliday, *Mao: The Unknown Story*, Vintage, 2006; p138 Chen Yun, 1979, quoted in P. Short, *Mao: A Life*, Murray, 2004; pp73, 105, 107, 114, 115(sources 2 and 3), 135 Nien Cheng, *Life and Death in Shanghai*, Grafton, 1986; p65 Chin Chao-yang, *Village Sketches*, 1957, quoted in J.Gittings, *The Changing Face of China*, OUP 2006; p21 From A. Cotterell, *China, A History*, Pimlico, 1988; pp74, 117 Anhua Gao, *To the Edge of the Sky*, Viking, 2000; pp57, 59, 83 From J. Horn, *Away With All Pests*, Hamlyn, 1969; p93 Lin Biao in the foreword to *Quotations from Chairman Mao*, Peking Foreign Language Press, 1966, quoted at www.marx2mao.com; p135 quoted in R. Macfarquhar, *The Politics of China*, Cambridge, 1993; pp15(sources 1, 2 and 3), 26, 27 (sources 5 and 6), 29, 31, 33, 41, 46(sources 2 and 3), 56, 61, 62, 68(sources 5 and 6), 71, 72(sources 8 and 9), 80(sources 3 and 4), 89, 90(sources 8, 9 and 10), 102(sources 4 and 5) From *Selected Works of Mao Tse-tung*, English edition, Peking Foreign Language Press, quoted at www.marx2mao.com; pp17, 18, 31 From J. F. Melby, *The Mandate of Heaven*, Chatto and Windus, 1968; p143 Adapted from Aiping Mu, *Vermilion Gate*, Abacus, 2000; pp96, 98, 110 Sirin Phathanothai, *The Dragon's Pearl*, Simon and Schuster/Pocket Books, 2006; pp52(sources 2 and 3), 84, 95, 104, 132, 139 P. Short, *Mao: A Life*, Murray, 2004; pp84, 127, 128, 142 J. D. Spence, *The Search for Modern China*, Norton, 1990; p59 S. Wood, *A Street in China*, 1958, quoted in J.Gittings, *The Changing Face of China*, OUP 2006; p142 Adapted from Wu Ningkun, *A Single Tear*, Hodder and Stoughton, 1993

Photographs courtesy of:

AFP/Getty Images: pp100, 101, 109; Edimedia: pp92, 113, 120, 121; Getty Liaison: p134; JEAN VINCENT/AFP/Getty Images: p105; KPA SIPA: p23; Courtesy of the IISH Stefan R. Landsberger Collection (http://www.iisg.nl): p136; Photo12 – Keystone: p115; Photos12.com – Oasis: pp34, 36, 51, 54, 56, 63, 65, 76, 106, 107, 108, 116, 118; Photo12.com – Oronoz: pp124, 141; Photos12.com – Panorama Stock: p30; Photo12.com – Ullstein Bild: pp11, 103; Photo12.com – Xinhua: pp14, 16, 21, 26, 32, 33, 43, 45, 49, 52, 67, 69, 74, 77, 78, 82, 83, 87, 88, 91, 123, 126, 133; Public domain: p132; Topfoto: pp01, 12, 18, 19, 27, 28, 39, 55, 70, 80, 96, 117, 128, 137; US National Library of Medicine: pp57, 58(top), 58(bottom);

Cover photography courtesy of Getty/ Jack Hollingsworth

Photo Research by Unique Dimension Ltd. www.uniquedimension.com

Grateful thanks are offered to Valery-Anne Giscard d'Estaing, Dora Swick, Ann Asquith and Samuel Manning for assistance with the Photo Research for this project.

Index